CONTENTS

Map references are denoted in the text by ❶ Central London ❷ West End
❸ Bus Map ❹ Tube Map ❺ Theatreland (p.29) ❻ Central London Overview

london places to see

London has to be the liveliest, grooviest, most enticing, most entertaining, most cosmopolitan city on Earth. 2,500 years in the making, it has everything the modern traveller could possibly want: superb architecture (St Paul's, the London Eye), a world-class arts scene (West End theatres, the South Bank), chic restaurants (The Ivy, the Oxo Tower) and fantastic shopping (Camden Market, Knightsbridge). There are ground-breaking museums (British Museum, Science Museum) and beautiful parks (St. James's Park, Hyde Park) – London boasts more green spaces than any other major capital. Culturally diverse, multi-racial and endlessly fascinating, London has a character and vibrancy not found anywhere else.

see it places to see

British Airways London Eye ❷6H

On a clear day, standing inside a huge glass egg at the top of the 450-ft London Eye, you can gaze over more than 25 miles of London's rooftops. Teetering on the south bank of the Thames by Westminster Bridge, the gently revolving spokes and 32 pod capsules make up the largest big wheel in the world. *Adm. Buy online for 10% discount. Open 10am-9pm daily Jun-Sept, 10am-8pm daily Oct-Apr (ticket office opens 9.30am). Jubilee Gardens SE1, T: 0870 500 0600, www.ba-londoneye.com*

British Museum ❷1G

Kids and adults alike flock here to see the huge Egyptian collection of ancient mummies and the Rosetta Stone. The famous Elgin Marbles from the Parthenon in Athens also reside here among hoards of world treasures collected by explorers. One of the highlights of this vast repository has to be the stunning glass-roofed Great Court, the largest covered public square in Europe. In its centre, have a peek at the beautiful blue and gold ceiling of the

The Great Court in the British Museum

huge round reading room. *Free. Open 10am-5.30pm daily (till 8.30pm Thu & Fri, Great Court open till 11pm Thu-Sat). Great Russell Street WC1, T: 020 7636 1555, www.thebritishmuseum.ac.uk*

Buckingham Palace ❷7D

Standing imperiously at the end of the Mall, this grand 19th-century structure is the official residence of the Queen. Each summer the Palace opens its doors to the public for guided tours of its state rooms (including the fabulous Royal Picture Gallery) and gardens. Don't miss the pageant of Englishness with the Changing of the Guard, which takes place daily in front of the palace at 11.27am Apr-Aug, alternate days Sep-Mar. *Adm. Open 9.45am-6pm daily (except some Saturdays) Aug-Sept(last entry 3.45pm). St. James's Park, T: 020 7766 7300, www.royalcollection.org.uk*

Camden Market ❶1D

Bustling with London's fashionistas, it is not uncommon to spot the odd celeb browsing among the vintage fashions, or stopping for coffee along the main street of London's famous Camden Town. Several markets make up this sprawling area: the principal ones being Camden Lock, housed in a restored Victorian building and specialising in arts and crafts; and the Stables, a vast Kasbah-like network of alleyways and railway arches off Chalk Farm Road, where you'll find an eclectic collection of memorabilia, posters, retro fashions, jewellery and antiques stalls. *Open 10am-6pm daily.* www.camdenlockmarket.com

Changing of the Guard at Buckingham Palace

Churchill Museum & Cabinet War Rooms ❷7F

Opened in 2005, this is the country's first museum dedicated to the great WWII leader, Sir Winston Churchill. It's set next to the underground bunkers that were both the British government's headquarters during the war. The map room, phone room and Sir Winston's bedroom have been preserved exactly as they were left at the end of the conflict. *Adm. Open 10am-6pm daily. Clive Steps, King Charles Street SW1, T: 020 7930 6961, cwr.iwm.org.uk*

Covent Garden ❷3H/❺

Weekends in Covent Garden are the busiest; once the site of a huge fruit and veg market, Covent Garden *(see p.18)* is now a lively, cosmopolitan centre of culture, creativity and cafes. Its former market buildings house an exciting mix of cool and quirky shops, restaurants, bars and museums (including the excellent London Transport Museum, *(see p.8)*), while its pedestrianised spaces attract huge crowds watching exuberant jugglers, acrobats, clowns and mime artists. www.coventgardenlife.com

Courtauld Gallery ❷3H

Home to the UK's most impressive collection of Impressionists including Monet, Manet, Renoir, Degas, Gauguin, Cézanne and Van Gogh, this intimate gallery also displays some superb works by Michelangelo, Botticelli and Rubens. Located at Somerset House *(see p.12)*. *Adm. Open 10am-6pm daily. Free entry 10am-2pm Mon. Somerset House WC2, T: 020 7848 2526,* www.courtauld.ac.uk/gallery

Dalí Universe ② 7H

Surreal bronze works by the Spanish artist, Salvador Dalí, are displayed in the County Hall Gallery. This is the largest collection of his sculptures in the world. On display are also some of his surreal hallucinatory images of melting clocks and dreamlike landscapes as well as his Mae West Lips sofa. *Adm. Open 10am-6.30pm daily. County Hall, Westminster Bridge Road SE1, T: 020 7450 7620, www.daliuniverse.com*

Dalí on the South Bank

Greenwich ① 6H

There are few more charming places in London than Greenwich. Set on the river, it's a town with a rich maritime history and a staggering architectural heritage. Christopher Wren, Nicholas Hawksmoor and Sir John Vanbrugh have all contributed to the Greenwich skyline, which has been designated a World Heritage Site by Unesco. Its status as the home of time – this is the site of the Prime Meridian or the line of 0° longitude at the Old Royal Observatory – led to it being picked as the venue for the nation's millennium celebrations. On Greenwich waterfront you can tour the *Cutty Sark*, one of the fastest tea clippers of the 19th century, standing in dry dock. At weekends, the bustling crafts or antiques markets *(see p.22)* attract visitors from all over. *T: 0870 608 2000, www.greenwich.gov.uk*

Houses of Parliament & Big Ben ② 7G

Laid out around Big Ben – its much-loved and over-photographed clocktower – the neo-gothic Palace of Westminster (as it's officially known) is the great icon of British democracy. Staring benignly across the river Thames, it's been the seat of government for centuries. The exquisitely preserved 11th-century Westminster Hall is all that remains of the early building. *To watch a debate from the House of Commons Visitors' Gallery, you must queue from 2.30pm onwards Mon-Wed, from 11.30am Thu and from 9.30am Fri. Guided tours of the building itself can only be taken during the summer recess from Jul-Sep. Book in advance. Parliament Square SW1, T: 020 729 3000 for tours, www.parliament.uk*

Hyde Park ② 3A-6A

Hyde Park, the city's green and pleasant heart, is London's largest open space. This grand expanse of grassy lawns, trees and flowerbeds is laid out around the Serpentine – a snaking, duck-filled lake – where rowboats can be hired. The Diana, Princess of Wales's controversial Memorial Fountain lies on the edge of Hyde Park next to Kensington Gardens (see right). In summer, the park comes to life with pop concerts and the BBC Proms (see p.61), open-air swimming at the lido and guided walks. Open 5am–midnight daily. www.royalparks.gov.uk

Imperial War Museum ❶ 5F
This excellent museum successfully strikes a balance between gung-ho displays of military hardware – tanks, planes and missiles – and exhibitions showing the human cost of war: check out the Trench Experience, the Blitz Experience and a new two-floor exhibition on the Holocaust. Free. Open 10am–6pm daily. Lambeth Road SE1, T: 020 746 5000, www.iwm.org.uk

Front Gates at Kensington Palace

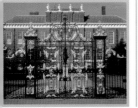

Kensington Gardens ❷ 3A-6A
This huge royal park was in fact part of Hyde Park (see p.6) until William III bought it in 1689 to live in and had Kensington Palace (see below) built. Next to the palace is a huge children's playground dedicated to the memory of Princess Diana, with a pirate ship and tepees. The Albert Memorial (see box, right) lies at the southern side of the gardens. Open 10am–dusk daily. www.royalparks.gov.uk

Kensington Palace ❶ 4B
The former home of the "People's Princess", Princess Diana, as well as the childhood home of Queen Victoria, houses a permanent collection of the grand Royal Ceremonial Dresses from 18th century to today. Until July 2007, Mario Testino's stunning photos of Diana are also on display. In the summer, the beautiful sunken gardens are a sight to behold. Adm. Open 10am–6pm daily Mar-Oct, 10am–5pm daily Oct-Mar. Kensington Gardens W8, T: 020 7937 9561, www.hrp.org.uk

Remembering Albert
During World War II, this grand, gaudy, gold-plated statue of Queen Victoria's beloved husband, Albert, was painted black to prevent it from being targeted by enemy planes. Sitting on the southern edge of Kensington Gardens, it has recently been returned to its former splendour.

Leicester Square ❷ 3F/❺

At the heart of London's entertainment district, Leicester Square hosts most of the UK film premieres in one of four cinemas (see p.34). Buy cut-price theatre tickets at the *tkts* booth (see box, p.28) in the corner. Wander a few streets into London's Chinatown and stop off for a bite to eat (see p.41), or check out the bars in Soho before dancing the night away in one of London's top nightspots back at the up-all-night Square.

Powder Blue Tang at the London Aquarium

London Aquarium ❷ 7H

Huge million-gallon tanks filled with tropical fish, seahorses and sharks now replace desks in County Hall, the former headquarters of the Greater London Council. The offices have been transformed into a state-of-the-art aquarium where a vast array of marine life now lives. The building also contains a museum dedicated to the great Spanish Surrealist, Salvador Dalí (see p.6). Adm. Open 10am-6pm daily (last admission 5pm). County Hall, Westminster Bridge Road SE1, T: 020 7967 8000, www.londonaquarium.co.uk

London Dungeon ❶ 4H

Gruesome dioramas and scary interactive exhibits combine in an overview of a gory historical past covering events such as the Great Plague and Jack the Ripper murders. The fairground-style attractions include the world's largest mirror maze. Adm. Book online for 30% reduction. Open 10am-6pm daily. 28-34 Tooley Street SE1, T: 020 7403 7221, www.thedungeons.com

London's Transport Museum ❷ 3H

Due to reopen in Spring 2007 after a

Saatchi Move ❶ 5D
Charles Saatchi is moving his acclaimed gallery of unseen, new contemporary art to the Duke of York's Headquarters on King's Road in Chelsea in 2007. T: 020 7823 2363, www.saatchi-gallery.co.uk

massive refurbishment, this lovely museum hides in the corner of Covent Garden. Charting the history of the capital's transport system with full-size old buses and tube trains, it is a must-see, even if you only buy your souvenirs from the excellent shop outside with underground station logo gifts and vintage transport posters (see p.24). Open 10am-6pm daily (11am Fri). Covent Garden Piazza WC2, T: 020 7379 6344, www.ltmuseum.co.uk

London Zoo ❶ 1D

The world's first 'scientific' zoo is home to a huge collection of animals from squirrel monkeys to elephants, giraffes, snakes, butterflies and parrots. Don't miss penguin

eeding time at 2.30pm daily. Look
out for the 'Web of Life' building, an
ncredible piece of architecture,
which shows how different animals
and organisms work together to
orm self-supporting eco-systems.
*Adm. Open 10am-5.30pm Mar-Oct,
10am-4pm Oct-Mar. Regent's Park
NW1, T: 020 7722 3333, www.zsl.org*

Canalboat to the Zoo
**The most pleasant way to
arrive at the zoo is aboard
a canal barge. The London
Waterbus Company organises
trips from Camden Lock to
Little Venice along Regent's
Canal, stopping at the zoo.**
*Apr-Sep, T: 020 7482 2660,
www.londonwaterbus.com*

Madame Tussauds & the London Planetarium ●2D

When Madame Tussaud arrived in
England from France in 1802
carrying with her a small collection
of wax masks modelled on the more
notorious victims of the French
Revolution, she could have had little
idea that some 200 years later a
waxwork museum bearing her name
would – with its high-kitsch blend of
celebrity likenesses and ghoulish
dioramas – have become one of the
country's most popular tourist
attractions. At the adjacent
Planetarium, you can see a hi-tech
presentation on the wonders of the
cosmos projected on to the ceiling
of its famous dome. *Adm. Open 9am-
5.30pm daily. Marylebone Road NW1,
T: 0870 400 3000, www.madame-
tussauds.com*

The Monument ●3H

Climb more than 300 spiral steps up
the 202-ft Doric column, designed
by Sir Christopher Wren in the 17th
century to commemorate the Great
Fire of London in 1666, for some
great views of the City of London.
202 feet significantly is also the
distance to the original bakery on
Pudding Lane where it is believed
the fire started. Some say the
monument is haunted by a woman
who jumped to her death from the
column – you may even feel her
ghost brush past you in her haste to
reach the top. *Adm. Open 9.30am-
5pm daily, Monument Street EC3,
T: 020 7626 2717.*

Museum of London ●3G

Opened in 1976 but recently
revamped, the museum explores the
development of the city over the
past 2,500 years – from prehistoric
camps to internet cafés. Look out for
The Lord Mayor of London's
ceremonial coach, which is still used
in the Lord Mayor's Show every year
(*see p.61*). *Free. Open 10am-6pm
Mon-Sat, noon-6pm Sun. London Wall
EC2, T: 020 7600 3699,
www.museum-london.org.uk*

Entrance to the Museum of London

Find the Famous

Follow in the footsteps of the famous; look out for blue plaques that adorn the sides of houses to indicate that someone famous lived there. High-profile former residents of London include John Fitzgerald Kennedy at 14 Princes Gate, Karl Marx at 28 Dean Street W1, Charles Dickens at 48 Doughty Street WC1, Oscar Wilde at 34 Tite Street SW3 and Nancy Astor (Britain's first female MP) at 4 James Square SW1.
www.blueplaque.com

National Gallery ❷ 4F/❺

The country's premier art gallery where more than 2,000 chronologically arranged paintings – works by da Vinci, Rembrandt, Constable, Van Gogh, Monet and Picasso – trace the development of western art from 13th-20th century. *Free. Open 10am-6pm (till 9pm Wed). Trafalgar Square WC2, T: 020 7747 2885, www.nationalgallery.org.uk*

National Portrait Gallery ❷ 4F/❺

Spend hours browsing more than 10,000 portraits from Tudor Kings and Queens to JK Rowling. The first-floor gallery displays depictions of modern icons in a variety of different styles and mediums, with superb pictures of the Kinnocks and Blur's famous greatest hits album cover. Recognised portraits from the earlier centuries include Shakespeare and Elizabeth I on the second floor. *Free. Open 10am-6pm daily (until 9pm Thu-Fri). 2 St Martin's Place WC2, T: 020 7312 2463, www.npg.org.uk*

Natural History Museum ❶ 5C

A colossal cathedral to nature whose

main draw is the 26-metre (78-ft) high diplodocus dinosaur skeleton. In addition to its two main sections, the Life Galleries (dinosaurs, mammals, birds) and the Earth Galleries (earthquakes, volcanoes, hurricanes), the museum boasts a shiny new Darwin Centre, a lecture hall-cum-laboratory where you can take behind-the-scenes tours. The museum also has an excellent kids' programme and free backpacks for the under sevens with explorer hat and binoculars. *Free. Open 10am-5.50pm Mon-Sat, Sun 11am-5.50pm. Cromwell Road SW7, T: 020 7942 5000, www.nhm.ac.uk*

Cruising the Thames

There is a relaxing and oft-overlooked way of getting around this hectic city: City Cruises operates a hop-on, hop-off ferry service (ask for a Rover ticket) stopping at Westminster Pier, Waterloo Pier, Tower Pier and Greenwich Pier. (*Daily, all year. T: 020 7740 0400, www.citycruises.com*). You can also take a leisurely cruise from Westminster Pier with Westminster Passenger Services upriver to Kew Gardens, Richmond and Hampton Court, south-west of the city centre. (*Apr-Oct. T: 020 7930 2062, www.wpsa.co.uk*)

James's Park ❷ 6D-6F

With its grand landscaping – the work of the great 17th-century French gardener André le Nôtre – and elegant lake which provides a home to a range of wildfowl, including swans, geese and even pelicans, this may well be the capital's most beautiful park. Bordered by the royal residences of Buckingham Palace (*see p.4*), St James's Palace (where Prince Charles lives) and Clarence House (the former home of the Queen Mother), it is a perfect spot to hire a deckchair and take a break from the bustle of London life. *Open 9am-dusk daily. www.royalparks.gov.uk*

St Paul's Cathedral ❶ 3G

Sir Christopher Wren's masterpiece was completed in the early 18th century and its great plump dome still dominates the city skyline. Though the façade is currently under wraps while it is restored ready for the building's 300th anniversary in 2008, the cathedral remains open to the public. There are 521 thigh-busting steps leading up to the topmost viewing gallery, from where you can enjoy great views out over the city. If the thought of climbing to the top leaves you puffed out, aim for the 259 steps that take you to the Whispering Gallery, where you can clearly hear the whispers from the other side of the gallery and the nave down below. *Adm. Open 8.30am-4pm Mon-Sat. St Paul's Churchyard EC4, T: 020 7236 4128, www.stpauls.co.uk*

St Paul's Cathedral

Science Museum ❶ 5C

From steam engines to computers, spinning jennies to rockets – the museum provides a complete overview of technological innovation over the centuries. The opening of the Wellcome Wing, with its hi-tech displays and Imax cinema, as well as the Dana Learning Centre where live science events are held, has helped to keep it on the cutting edge. Superb hands-on exhibits, such as building bridges, will keep the kids happy for hours. *Free. Open 10am-6pm daily. Exhibition Road SW7, T: 020 7942 4000, www.sciencemuseum.org.uk*

Shakespeare's Globe ❶ 4G

This full-scale recreation of the Shakespearean theatre, built using traditional materials and methods, is very near the spot where the original Globe burnt down in 1613. Choose to watch a performance sitting on a wooden seat (bring or hire a cushion) or suffer as the average Elizabethan would have done, and stand in the open-air yard in front of the stage (they sell plastic macs in the shop should it rain). There's also a multimedia exhibition of the theatre's history. *Open 9am-4pm Sep-May, 10am-5pm Oct-Apr, call well in advance for performance times. Bear Gardens, Bankside SE1, T: 020 7902 1500, www.shakespeares-globe.org*

Sherlock Holmes Museum ❶ 2C

Located in the fictional detective's address, this museum to Arthur Conan Doyle's most famous

The whole world's a stage: Shakespeare's Globe

character resembles the Victorian interior of the investigator's home complete with deerstalker, pipe and slippers as described by the author. Actors take up the roles of Sherlock Holmes, Doctor Watson and Mrs Hudson. *Adm. Open 9.30am-6pm daily. 221b Baker Street NW1, T: 020 7935 8866, www.sherlock-holmes.co.uk*

Somerset House ❷ 4H

Enjoy the architectural splendour of this grand mansion, built in the late 18th century to replace a derelict Tudor palace. Stroll through the shooting fountains in its courtyard with special shows every half hour, admire its grand river views and visit its three prestigious collections: the Courtauld Gallery (*see p.5*), the Gilbert Collection of Decorative Arts and the Hermitage Rooms. At Christmas, a temporary ice-skating rink is set up in the courtyard. *Free entry to courtyard and river terrace. Open 10am-6pm daily. Courtyard open later. The Strand WC, T: 020 7845 4600, www.somerset-house.org.uk*

South Bank & Bankside ❷ 4F-4G

Strolling along the south bank of the Thames is a pleasant way to spend a few hours. Starting from Westminster Pier pass the London Eye (see p.4), until you reach the Royal Festival Hall and South Bank Centre, where on Friday evenings you can catch a free, live jazz concert (see box p.32). The waterside teems with life, especially at the weekend with a secondhand book market held every Sunday morning under Waterloo Bridge. Stop off at Gabriel's Wharf, a small, delightful complex of artisans' shops and riverside restaurants, before heading towards the landmark Oxo tower, a former power station acquired by the Oxo company, with its shops and restaurants (see p.40). For the more adventurous, carry on to the Tate Modern (see right) and Shakespeare's Globe (see left) at Bankside. www.southbanklondon.com

Tate Britain ❶ 5E

Now that its mind-blowing modern art collection has moved to the Tate Modern (see right), the old Tate is free to concentrate on what it does best – showcasing British talent throughout the ages. All the great British names are here – Constable, Gainsborough, Hogarth, Epstein, Spencer, Stubbs, Hockney, Moore and Turner – in what is undoubtedly the country's greatest heritage to a fantastic heritage of domestic art.
Free. Open 10am-6pm daily. Millbank SW1, T: 020 7887 8000, www.tate.org.uk

Tate Modern ❶ 4G

Lavished with praise on its opening, this former monolithic power station

Former power station: Tate Modern

Tate à Tate

Take the catamaran, with a Damien Hirst designed livery, which shuttles between both Tate galleries (see below) with a stop at the London Eye (see p.4) every 40 minutes. Buy tickets from Tate galleries, phone or online.
T: 020 7887 8888, www.tate.org.uk/tatetotate

in Bankside is now firmly established as one of Europe's leading modern art galleries. With works by the likes of Picasso, Rothko and Pollock on permanent display, it also plays host to a succession of high-profile temporary exhibitions, and extra-large one-off displays in its cathedral-like Turbine Hall. Enjoy fantastic views of St Paul's (see p.11), the Thames and the Millennium Bridge from the fifth floor and the museum's Level Seven café. *Free. Open 10am-6pm (till 10pm Fri & Sat). Bankside SE1, T: 020 7887 8000, www.tate.org.uk*

Tower Bridge ❶ 4H

After Big Ben (*see p.6*), this great pinnacled bridge, finished in 1894, is perhaps the most photographed structure in all London. On the Tower Bridge Experience you can learn how its mighty decks are raised (when a large vessel comes upriver) and take a walk along one of the two covered walkways at the top of the bridge, which offer great views up and down the Thames. *Open 9.30am-6pm daily. Tower Hill EC3, T: 020 7403 3761, www.towerbridge.org.uk*

Kids having fun at Tower Bridge

Tower of London ❶ 4H

The Crown Jewels, including the sparkling Coronation Crown and mace, are guarded by the resident Yeoman Warders, commonly known as the Beefeaters. Also acting as guides, try to catch one of their informative tours. Constructed on the orders of William the Conqueror, the tower has stood guard over the city for nearly 1,000 years. It was used as a prison during the Middle Ages and its more illustrious captives included Anne Boleyn, the hapless second wife of Henry VIII and the two princes murdered on the orders

The Tower of London

of Richard III. *Adm. Open 9am-6pm Tue-Sat, 10am-6pm Sun-Mon Mar-Oct, 9am-5pm Tue-Sat, 10am-5pm Sun-Mon Nov-Feb. Tower Hill EC3, T: 0870 756 6060, www.hrp.org.uk*

Victoria & Albert Museum ❶ 5C

Large, rambling and somewhat confusingly laid out, the grand V&A South Kensington is nonetheless the city's finest collection of decorative arts. Its nine km (seven miles) of galleries hold a treasure trove of silverware, costumes, sculptures, paintings, ceramics and porcelain. Collections include fashion from the

Victoria and Albert Museum

...7th century to the present day ...cluding 20th century designers ...uch as Mary Quant and Vivienne ...Westwood, contemporary graphic ...rts, and modern-life ephemera from ...he telephone through to the ipod. *...ree. Open 10am-5.45pm (Wed & last ...i monthly till 10pm). Cromwell Road ...W7, T: 020 7942 2000, ...ww.vam.ac.uk*

Westminster Abbey ❶ 5E

...ow a hot destination on the Da ...inci Code grand tour, this Gothic ...bbey is a memorial to the nation, ...lled with the tombs of the country's greatest monarchs, politicians, poets, scientists and musicians. Look out for the Coronation Chair, on which all but one of Britain's monarchs have been crowned since 1308. On Sundays at 5.45pm enjoy the free organ recital. *Adm. Open 9.30am-3.45pm Mon-Fri (till 7pm on Wed), 9.30am-1.45pm Sat. Dean's Yard SW1, T: 020 7654 4900, www.westminster-abbey.org*

Westminster Cathedral ❶ 5E

Built in Byzantine style, this ornate Catholic church was completed in the early 20th century, with a dome and soaring belltower made of red brick with white stripes. The nave is the widest of any church in England and you can see the High Altar from all seats. Try to catch the sublime voices of the Westminster Cathedral Choir who sing daily Mass and Vespers, with concerts every second Tuesday from June until September. *Free. Open 7am-7pm daily. Viewing Gallery open 9.30am-12.30pm & 1pm -5pm daily. 42 Francis Street SW1, T: 020 7798 9055, www.westminstercathedral.org.uk*

Altar inside Westminster Abbey

london places to shop

Shopping heaven: from antique markets where you can hunt for bargains at the crack of dawn to world-famous department stores, chic boutiques filled with high fashions to labyrinthine bookshops and vast music emporiums, London is a city made for spending. Indeed, the shopping bug has grown so strong in the capital that many of its best shopping areas, such as Oxford Street (with four tube stations along its length), Knightsbridge (home to Harrods and Harvey Nichols) and Covent Garden (plus its surrounding streets full of funky stores), as well as the markets at Camden Lock and Portobello Road, have become tourist attractions in their own right.

buy it places to shop

Shopping Areas

Carnaby Street ❷ 3D

Once part of 60s' Swinging London (see also King's Road, right), the area became run down and so has been beautifully redeveloped into a wide pedestrianised street with small independent clothes stores and bright, clean modern shops selling funky sports, surf and ski wear. Neighbouring Kingly Street has some lovely little shops and cafés; also take a peek at the stores in Kingly Court, a three-floor former timber warehouse with courtyard.
www.carnaby.co.uk

Charing Cross Road ❷ 2F-4F/❺

The area for book browsing, where you'll find several of the big names – Blackwell's, Borders, Foyles (see p.23), Waterstone's – surrounded by a cluster of secondhand book stores.

Covent Garden ❷ 3H/❻

The former fruit-and-veg market area (see p.5) is now a thriving centre of culture and commerce. Apple Market and Jubilee Market sell antiques, handicrafts, handmade jewellery, gems, clothes and souvenirs. Around the piazza, stock up on some of the high-street labels, or take a wander into the surrounding Floral Street, Neal Street, Monmouth Street and Seven Dials for funky little stores selling everything from tea, shoes and tarot cards, to unique, trendy clothes and organic food and cosmetics. www.coventgardenlife.com

Jermyn Street ❷ 5D-4E

Lined with shops that seem to be inhabiting some sort of timewarp, Jermyn Street is where the refined English gentleman can be found buying his tailored suits, collared shirts and Cuban cigars.

Shopping in Covent Garden Piazza

King's Road ❶ 6B-5D

The centre of 1960s 'Swinging London' is still going strong. Expect chic boutiques, smart restaurants, pavement cafés, exclusive antique shops and lots of well-groomed people parading up and down.

Knightsbridge ❶ 4C

The home of British haute couture, Knightsbridge is the shopping area of choice for fashion-conscious people with money to burn. Boasting the capital's two most well-to-do stores – Harrods and

Harvey Nichols *(see p.20)* – its streets (particularly Brompton Road, Sloane Street, Beauchamp Place) are lined with designer-clothes stores.

Old & New Bond Streets ❷ 2C-4D
One of the most exclusive shopping streets in London, Bond Street is a mecca for high-fashion designers and their celeb clients: Chanel, Donna Karan, Versace, D&G, Gucci, Jimmy Choo; and jewellery: Cartier and Graff. It's also home to two of the city's most prestigious auction houses, Sotheby's and Phillips.

Oxford & Regent Streets ❷ 3A-4D
For many people, these two equal bisecting shopping streets are the very essence of London, hence the huge swarming crowds that congregate here every weekend, especially at Oxford Circus. Oxford Street is lined with department stores: M&S, John Lewis, Selfridges, Debenhams, House of Fraser *(see p.24)*, big-name chains and cheap and cheerful souvenir stalls, while sweeping Regent Street is a touch more elegant, possessing graceful architecture and genteel choices:

Liberty's *(see p.20)* and Laura Ashley, mixed in with state-of-the-art shops such as the Apple Store.

Savile Row ❷ 4D
Lined with upmarket tailors and gentlemen's outfitters, Savile Row represents an old-fashioned bastion of hand-stitched, made-to-measure luxury tweeds and suiting for both ladies and gents.

Tottenham Court Road ❷ 1F
In amongst a smattering of upmarket interior design stores and high-street shops, you can pick up a bargain in one of the electronic and computer goods retailers.

Department Stores

Fortnum & Mason ❷ 4D
Elegant and refined or stuffy and old-fashioned (depending on how you look at things), Fortnums prides itself on its status as a conveyor of comestibles to the aristocracy. Its justly famous tea hall is on the ground floor *(see p.25)*. 181 Piccadilly

W1, T: 020 7734 8040,
www.fortnumandmason.co.uk

Harrods ❶ 5C
A national institution, sometimes subsumed beneath the gargantuan personality of its owner, Mohammed Al-Fayed, Harrods is still London's pre-eminent department store. With a mighty 4.5 acres of floor space, the

Harrods by night

shop stocks everything from fashion to pets, toys to sporting goods. Its magnificent 17-department food halls are the one of the highlights as well as the Egyptian Hall on the Lower Ground and Ground floors and the Egyptian-themed escalators which run through the centre of the store. *87-135 Brompton Road SW1, T: 020 7730 1234, www.harrods.com*

Harvey Nichols ❶ 4C

'Harvey Nics' is Harrods' younger, groovier sibling. Smaller and with a narrower range of goods, it is best known for its designer clothes and fabulous food hall. *109-125 Knightsbridge SW1, T: 020 7235 5000, www.harveynichols.com*

Hunt Down a Bargain

Large-scale sales at the city's department stores (where reductions of 50% or greater are commonplace) take place twice a year in January and July. The most famous are held by Harrods (*see p.19*), when huge crowds descend on the store hunting for the ultimate bargain.

House of Fraser ❷ 2C

A mid-size department store specialising in mid-range fashions – Rive Gauche, Burberry, Jasper Conran and so on – at medium prices. Good for coats and cosmetics. *318 Oxford Street W1, T: 0870 160 7258, www.houseoffraser.co.uk*

John Lewis ❷ 2C

Don't go expecting high fashions; this is a no-nonsense kind of a place. It's particularly good for housewares, haberdashery and ready-to-wear clothes. *278-30 Oxford Street W1, T: 020 7629 7711, www.johnlewis.co.uk*

Liberty ❷ 3D

Housed in a lovely Tudor-style building, Liberty has an artsy-craftsy sort of vibe with very good fashion and furniture departments – its printed scarves find their way into a million parcels come Christmas. *210-20 Regent Street W1, T: 020 7734 1234, www.liberty.co.uk*

Marks & Spencer ❷ 2A-3A

M&S is a formidable British institution and still the place for

Liberty at sale time

Portobello Road Market

ready-made meals and quality, affordable underwear. Recently, the M&S branded clothes underwent a major style overhaul and its new stylish range of Per Una hangs in many a modern British woman's wardrobe. **Main branch**: *458 Oxford Street W1, T: 020 7935 7954, www.marksandspencer.com*

Peter Jones ❶ 5D

Considering its location and typically Chelsea-Belgravia clientele, much of the merchandise at Peter Jones (part of the John Lewis group) is surprisingly affordable. Posh yet homey, it's good for linens and fabric. *Sloane Square SW1, T: 020 7730 3434, www.peterjones.co.uk*

Selfridges ❷ 2B

Much more lively and vibrant following its recent £100m makeover, there's still something maze-like about Selfridges. It is big, with a huge range of goods on offer, and some excellent places to stop for a bite to eat. *400 Oxford Street W1, T: 0870 837 7377, www.selfridges.co.uk*

Markets

Bermondsey Market ❶ 4H

This antiques market appears Brigadoon-like every Friday morning. Get up early – the bargains have gone by 9am. *Open 4am-3pm Fri. Bermondsey Square SE1.*

Berwick Street Market ❷ 3E

Berwick Street Market is an excellent source of good quality fruit and veg, cheese, bread and spices, and has an old-fashioned feel to it. *Open 8am-6pm Mon-Sat. Berwick Street, Soho W1.*

Brick Lane Market ❶ 2H

Taste local life in this typical East End market selling cheap household goods, clothes and bits and pieces of tatty jewellery. *Open 8am-2pm Sun. Brick Lane E1, www.eastlondonmarkets.com*

Borough Market ❶ 4G

Recently voted one of London's 'Favourite Day's Out', this is a real foodies' market with a fabulous selection of meats, fish, vegetables, fruit, exotic cheeses, bread, coffee and spices. *Open 12pm-6pm Fri, 9am-*

4pm Sat. Southwark Street SE1,
T: 020 7407 1002,
www.boroughmarket.org.uk

Camden Market ● 1D

See p.4.

Columbia Road Market ● 1H

Start your Sunday morning in this lovely, vibrant flower market with stalls filled with colourful blooms, shrubs, bedding plants and, come December, Christmas trees and mistletoe. It's a trek by tube but worth the effort. *Open 8am-2pm Sun. Columbia Road E2, www.eastlondonmarkets.com*

Columbia Road Flower Market

Greenwich Market ● 6H

Greenwich (*see p.6*) is home to three separate markets – a crowded antiques market (off Greenwich High Road), a covered craft market (College Approach), and a sprawling central market (Stockwell Street) selling second-hand clothes, books and furniture. *Open 7.30am-5pm Thu, 9.30am-5pm Fri-Sun. www.greenwich-market.co.uk*

Petticoat Lane Market ● 3H

A cheery, honest-to-goodness street market specialising in cheap fashion, knock-off goods, jewellery and second-hand tat. *Open 9am-2pm Sun-Fri. Middlesex Street E1, www.eastlondonmarkets.com*

Portobello Road Market ● 3A

Popular flea-market and stores with everything from antiques and vintage clothes, to fruit and veg and household goods. **General Market** *Open 8am-6pm Mon-Sat (1pm Thu),* **Antique Market** *Open 5.30am-5pm Sat. Portobello Road, Notting Hill W10, T: 020 7229 8354, www.portobelloroad.co.uk*

Antiques

Antiquarius ● 6C

Over a hundred stalls selling a vast range of antiques, memorabilia and (for want of a better word) junk. *131-141 King's Road SW3, T: 020 7351 5353, www.antiquarius.co.uk*

Silver and antiques at the market

Astrology

The Astrology Shop ❷ 2G

Refresh your spiritual supplies from a large choice of tarot cards, crystals, and incense sticks.
78 Neal Street, Covent Garden WC2, T: 020 7813 3051, www.londonastrology.com

Book Shops

Borders ❷ 2D

This giant three-floor book, CD and DVD emporium organises regular events – book signings, storytellings

Stanfords is famous for maps and guidebooks

for kids – and is good for periodicals.
203 Oxford Street W1, T: 020 7292 1600, www.borders.com

Foyle's ❷ 2F/❺

Foyle's astonishingly eclectic layout is the stuff of legend. With copious amounts of titles, it's famed for stocking the stuff other stores don't.
113-119 Charing Cross Road WC2, T: 020 7437 5660, www.foyles.co.uk

Stanfords ❷ 3G/❺

London's premier map and travel-guide book shop. *12-14 Long Acre WC2, T: 020 7836 1321, www.stanfords.co.uk*

Waterstone's ❷ 4E/❺

This branch is the largest bookshop in Europe, with a fifth-floor café and bar with views of the capital. *203-206 Piccadilly W1, T: 020 7851 2400, www.waterstones.co.uk*

Cosmetics

B ❷ 3D

Step into the gorgeous boudoir-style emporium filled with shelves of beautifully coloured beaded perfume

bottles and atomisers. This aladdin's cave of smellies is the upmarket version of Lush, the handmade cosmetics company.
39 Carnaby Street W1, T: 020 7287 5492, www.bnevertoobusytobebeautiful.com

B's luscious selection of cosmetics

The Sanctuary ❷ 3G

Stop off for a bit of pampering after a hard days' shopping frenzy, and relax in a fluffy robe around the pool or treat yourself to some of the blissful products in the store.
12 Floral Street, Covent Garden WC2, T: 0870 770 3350, www.thesanctuary.co.uk

SEN  2C

In amongst the Chinese medicines and herbal teas, you can find some beautifully designed and exquisite smelling skin and body products, including a whole range of bath gels and body scrubs to promote weight loss (if you should require). 59 South Molton Street W1, T: 020 7629 2243, www.senhealth.com

Designer Fashion

Burberry 3D

The oh-so-British and world-favourite Burberry plaid adorns coats, scarves, perfumes and bags. *21-23 New Bond Street W1, T: 020 7839 5222, www.burberry.com*

Matthew Williamson 2E

One of the latest celeb-designers, his modern, fresh, feminine clothes are renowned for bright colours and unique prints. *28 Bruton Street W1, T: 020 7629 6200, www.matthewwilliamson.com*

Paul Smith 2E

This very English designer owns a couple of stores in Covent Garden selling his trademark shirts and own-brand designer fragrances. *40/44 Floral Street WC2, T: 020 7379 7133, www.paulsmith.co.uk*

Discount

Brown's Labels for Less 3C

Permanently low sale prices on designer labels, as well as discounted Brown's Own fashions for men and women. *50 South Molton Street W1, T: 020 7514 0052, www.brownsfashion.com*

Museum Shops

British Museum Store 1F

For unique gifts based on the exhibits, the British Museum (*see p.4*) shop stocks ideal souvenirs and educational toys from Egyptian Mummy key rings to scarves and intricate jigsaws. *Great Court, British Museum, Great Russell Street WC1, T: 020 7637 1292, www.britishmuseum.co.uk*

London's Transport Museum 2E

London gifts embossed with the underground logo prove a popular souvenir – treat the kids to an Angel Station t-shirt. The shop also stocks one of the most comprehensive ranges of vintage transport posters around. *Unit 26, Covent Garden Piazza (until Summer 2007, when it returns to the museum see p.8), T: 020 7379 6344, www.ltmuseumshop.co.uk*

Music

HMV 🎵 2E
Huge entertainment supermarket with vast stocks of videos, DVDs, CDs and computer games.
*150 Oxford Street W1,
T: 020 7631 3423, www.hmv.co.uk*

Virgin Megastore 🎵 1F
Supposedly London's largest record shop, the Virgin Megastore boasts a comprehensive classical music section. *14 Oxford Street W1 plus other locations, T: 020 7631 1234, www.virgin.com*

Parfumerie

Penhaligon's 🎵 4D
Perfumier to the Queen, this tiny store in the Burlington Arcade, stocks a huge bouquet of own-fragrances and sweet-smelling soaps.
16 Burlington Arcade W1, T: 020 7629 1416, www.penhaligons.co.uk

Sporting Goods

Lillywhites 🎵 4E
Long-term sporting staple store occupying a corner of Piccadilly Circus. Sells tennis rackets, skis, footballs and designer sportswear.
*24-36 Lower Regent Street SW1,
T: 0870 333 9600,
www.sports-world.com*

Tea

Fortnum & Mason 🎵 4D
Tea, tea and more tea – this very British drink has more flavours than ice cream in the most famous tea hall of all (*see p.19*). *181 Piccadilly W1, T: 020 7734 8040, www.fortnumandmason.co.uk*

Toys

Benjamin Pollock's Toy Shop 🎵 3G
Olde-Worlde toys and games: a delightful, cramped first-floor shop full of puppets, kaleidoscopes and intricate paper theatres.
*44 Covent Garden Market WC2,
T: 020 7379 7866,
www.pollockscoventgarden.co.uk*

Hamleys 🎵 3D
The country's most famous toy store – and perhaps the most crowded (and noisy) place on earth – Hamleys boasts five floors of toys, board games, teddy bears and computer games. *188-96 Regent Street W1, T: 0870 333 2455, www.hamleys.com*

Hamleys is child heaven

london entertainment

It's easy to be entertained in London. Everyday, the city plays host to hundreds of shows, plays, concerts, films, recitals and comedy performances. Major sporting events such as the London Marathon, Oxford-Cambridge Boat Race, Wimbledon Tennis Championships and Premier League football matches take place throughout the year as do themed film seasons at places like the National Film Theatre (not to mention numerous star-laden Leicester Square premieres). With an unrivalled theatrical heritage, thriving music scene, superb sporting facilities, state-of-the-art cinemas and world-class arts venues such as the Royal Opera House, Barbican and South Bank Complex, it's little wonder that the city acts as a magnet for the world's greatest entertainers and performers.

watch it entertainment

What's On

For entertainment listings, the weekly entertainment magazine *Time Out* is an invaluable source, as is the *Evening Standard's Metro Life* supplement (published Thursdays) as well as *The Guide*, free with *The Guardian's* Saturday edition. London Tourist Board operates an information hotline:
T: 0905 766 011 (70p a minute), (from overseas: +44 870 345 9898).

You can also check out the following:
www.londontouristboard.com
www.londontown.com
www.thisislondon.co.uk
www.timeout.co.uk

Tickets

Buy tickets direct from the venue – box offices are open 10am-8pm, or:

Society of London Theatre Guide
Operates the *tkts* Booth on Leicester Square (*see box, right*) for discounted on-the-day theatre tickets.
T: 020 7557 6700,
www.officiallondontheatre.co.uk

Cheap Tickets
Fancy seeing a show, but don't want to pay through the nose? Head down to the *tkts* booth (**2** 4F/**5**) on Leicester Square which sells half-price tickets for West End shows on a first-come, first-served basis. It's four tickets per person max and a £2.50 booking fee.
Open 10am-7pm Mon-Sat, 12pm-3pm Sun.
www.officiallondontheatre.co.uk

Ticketline
T: 0870 444 5556,
www.ticketline.com

Ticketmaster
T: 0870 534 4444,
www.ticketmaster.co.uk

Major Venues

Theatre
With more than 40 commercial theatres staging anything from experimental comedies to Shakespearean tragedies by way of all-singing, all-dancing long-running musical extravaganzas, London's West End theatre scene is justifiably one of the most famous and well-respected in the world.

Top Shows

Chicago **2** 2G/**6**
This award-winning musical has been in the West End since 1997 and is still going strong. *Cambridge Theatre, Seven Dials WC2, T: 0870 890 1102,* www.chicagothemusical.com

The Lion King **2** 3H/**6**
Disney's superb story of Simba the lion with Elton John's excellent musical score and award-winning puppets and costumes.
Lyceum, 21 Wellington Street WC2, T: 0870 243 9000, www.thelionking.co.uk

Mamma Mia **2** 4F/**6**
Abba's fantastic feel-good music set around the story of a girl seeking her father's identity. *Prince of Wales Theatre, Coventry Street W1, T: 0870 850 0393,* www.mamma-mia.com

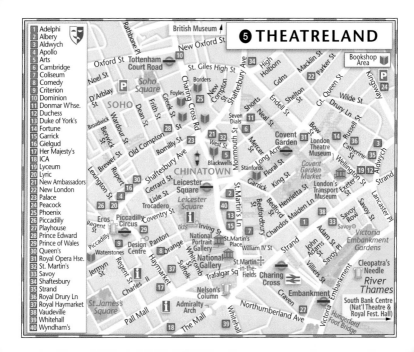

Les Misérables ❷ 3F/❺

Based on Victor Hugo's novel the operatic marvel of 'Les Mis', as it's more commonly known, is produced by Cameron Mackintosh. *Queen's Theatre, 51 Shaftesbury Avenue W1, T: 0870 950 0930, www.lesmis.com*

Phantom of the Opera ❷ 5F/❺

Andrew Lloyd Webber's stunning musical love story set in the Paris Opera. *Her Majesty's Theatre, Haymarket SW1, T: 0870 534 4444, www.thephantomoftheopera.com*

We Will Rock You ❷ 1F

Join in Queen's foot-stomping rock anthems, scripted by Ben Elton. *Dominion Theatre, Tottenham Court Road W1, T: 0870 169 0116, www.queenonline.com/wewillrockyou*

Individual Theatres

National Theatre ❶ 4F

One of the country's great theatrical complexes, the state-sponsored National boasts three auditoriums (in descending size): the Olivier, the Lyttelton and the Cottesloe, where you can see everything from big budget musicals such as *Guys and Dolls* and *Jerry Springer: The Opera* to new work by gifted young playwrights. *South Bank SE1, T: 020 7452 3000, www.nt-online.org*

Royal Court ❶ 5D

This prestigious venue – which makes a point of commissioning and staging edgy, challenging writing – has undergone a £25m refit restoring its theatres, named 'Upstairs' and 'Downstairs', to their former glory. *Sloane Square SW1, T: 020 7565 5000, www.royalcourttheatre.com*

Outside the National Theatre

Shakespeare's Globe ❶ 4G

Experience 'authentic' Shakespearean performances at this re-creation of the Elizabethan venue where the audiences heckle the actors. For more details, *see p.12.*

Old Vic Theatre ❶ 4F

Though the first productions of new artistic director, Kevin Spacey, met with a mixed critical reception, the presence of the great Hollywood actor undoubtedly draws in the crowds. Recent audience-pulling productions include *Richard II* and *The Philadelphia Story*. Be sure to book early. *Waterloo Road SE1, T: 0870 060 6628, www.oldvictheatre.com*

Regent's Park Open Air Theatre ❶ 2D

Now that the RSC has decamped from the Barbican, this is one of the best places to see the Bard's work performed. Start with a picnic in the park (*see p.60*) and then take your seat for a night of alfresco drama. *Regent's Park NW1, T: 0870 060 1811, www.openairtheatre.org*

Music & Ballet

Barbican Centre ❶ 3H

Almost universally derided as an ugly modernist eyesore, the Barbican compensates for any aesthetic deficiencies with the quality of its facilities, which include performance spaces, theatres and cinemas. It's home to the London Symphony Orchestra and hosts performances by the BBC Symphony Orchestra

The Royal Albert Hall

and City of London Symphonia. *Silk Street EC2, T: 020 7638 8891, www.barbican.org.uk*

Holland Park Theatre ❶ 4A

Watch the Royal Ballet dance under the stars or listen to the peacocks in the park (*see p.60*) trying to outdo the opera singers, with the ruins of Holland House as an exquisite backdrop. Open-air performances only run in the summer months and are extremely popular so book well in advance. *Holland Park W8, T: 0845 230 9769, www.operahollandpark.com*

London Coliseum ❷ 3G/❺

The recently refurbished home of the English National Opera aims to bring 'opera to the masses', with some ticket prices for midweek performances available for as little as £10. *St Martin's Lane WC1, T: 0845 145 0200, www.eno.org*

Royal Albert Hall ❶ 4B

This 19th-century barrel-shaped venue stages a high-profile series of classical concerts, the Proms (*see p.61*), from mid-July to mid-September,

culminating in an evening in which patriots belt out 'Rule Britannia'. *Kensington Gore SW7, T: 020 7589 8212, www.royalalberthall.com*

The Royal Opera House

Royal Opera House ❷ 3G/❺

The home of the Royal Opera and Royal Ballet is one of the sparkling jewels in the capital's classical music crown. Free concerts and exhibitions are held in the Floral Hall. *Covent Garden WC2, T: 020 7304 4000, www.royaloperahouse.org.uk*

South Bank Centre ❷ 5H

This vast concrete monument to stark functionalism has been 'about to be revamped' for more than a decade and is still waiting for a donor to come along. Although a bit creaky around the edges, it's a great place to hear classical music with three celebrated venues – the **Royal Festival Hall**, the **Queen Elizabeth Hall** and the **Purcell Room**. *South Bank SE1, T: 0870 380 4300, www.rfh.org.uk
www.southbankcentre.org.uk*

Wigmore Hall ❶ 1C

A small, well-respected art nouveau concert hall – with wonderful acoustics – which specialises in

Free Music

Relax over lunch with a free classical concert held at St. Martin-in-the-Fields church (❷ 4G) on Mon, Tue & Fri at 1.05pm. On Friday evenings at 5.15pm, catch a free jazz performance at the Queen Elizabeth Hall (❷ 5H) in the South Bank Centre (*see above*).

chamber music and solo pianist performances. *35 Wigmore Street W1, T: 020 7935 2141, www.wigmore-hall.org.uk*

Sadler's Wells ❶ 1F

Now refurbished, this is one of the best places to see contemporary dance productions. *Rosebery Avenue EC1, T: 0870 737 7737, www.sadlers-wells.com*

Rock & Pop

Carling Academy Brixton (off map)

Groovy, sweaty, all-standing venue popular with up-and-comers and big stars (Madonna, the Stones). The sloping floor allows great views, even from the back. *211 Stockwell Road, Brixton SW9, T: 0870 060 0100, www.brixton-academy.co.uk*

Earl's Court Exhibition Centre ❶ 6A

This vast exhibition centre (home to the annual Boat Show and the Ideal Home Exhibition) also hosts major league acts like U2, Madonna and Justin Timberlake. *Warwick Road, Earl's Court SW5, T: 020 7385 1200, www.eco.co.uk*

Dingwalls ❶ 1D

Part of the vibrant Camden scene, Dingwalls puts on rock, pop and indie acts five days a week. On Fridays and Saturdays it transforms into the **Jongleurs Comedy Club** (*see right*). *Middle Yard, Camden Lock NW1, T: 020 7428 5929, www.dingwall.com*

Mean Fiddler ❷ 3F

An intimate venue that attracts both established pop and rock acts as well as unsigned bands. Rock on Fridays is the biggest rock night in London. *165 Charing Cross Road WC2, T: 0870 060 3777, www.meanfiddler.com*

Jazz

Jazz Café ❶ 1D

Owned by the Mean Fiddler Group (*see above*), this restaurant venue showcases funk, soul and folk as well as traditional and modern jazz. *5 Parkway, Camden NW1, T: 0870 150 0044, www.jazzcafe.co.u*

Pizza Express Jazz Club ❷ 2E

A Soho institution – live jazz is serve

...ve music with no pretensions

...p in the basement most weekends. *...0 Dean Street W1, T: 020 7439 8722, ...ww.pizzaexpress.co.uk*

...onnie Scott's ❷ 2F

...he most famous jazz venue of them ...l – all the greats have played here. ...deed, to get a slot at Ronnie ...cott's is very much a rite of passage ...r any aspiring jazz performer. ...mokey and cool. *47 Frith Street W1, ... 020 7439 0747, ...ww.ronniescotts.co.uk*

...00 Club ❷ 1E

...t the vanguard of the punk ...evolution in the late 1970s, these ...ays the 100 Club tends to focus on

quieter, less angry fare – jazz, soul, funk and so on. *100 Oxford Street W1, T: 020 7636 0933, www.the100club.co.uk*

Comedy

Comedy Café ❶ 2H

This purpose-built comedy venue, brightly decorated and always crowded, provides a regular turnover of new and established acts. There is a late bar, reasonable food and dancing as well as the standup. *Open 7pm Wed-Sat. 66 Rivington Street EC2, T: 020 7739 5706, www.comedycafe.co.uk*

Cheery façade of the Comedy Café

Comedy Store ❷ 4F

The granddaddy of all comedy venues, the Store, which opened in the late '70s, attracts all the top stars – Rik Mayall, Dawn French and Robin Williams; the Comedy Store Players, provide improvised hilarity on Wednesdays and Sundays. *Haymarket House, 1a Oxendon Street SW1, T: 0870 534 4444 (Ticketmaster), www.thecomedystore.co.uk*

Jongleurs ❶ 1C

The Jongleurs Group run high-quality comedy evenings at four separate venues across London at Battersea, Bow, Camden and Watford. *T: 0870 787 0707, www.jongleurs.com*

Cinema

BFI London Imax Cinema ❶ 4F
3D-extravaganzas are projected on to the biggest screen in Britain at this state-of-the-art facility housed in a stunning cylindrical building near Waterloo Station. *1 Charlie Chaplin Walk, South Bank SE1, T: 0870 787 2525, www.bfi.org.uk/imax*

London Imax lights up at night

Empire ❷ 3F
Leicester Square WC2, T: 08714 714 714, www.empirecinemas.co.uk

National Film Theatre ❶ 4F
With more than 2,000 films – made up of classics, British rarities, foreign work and archived TV – shown each year, the NFT offers the most diverse cinematic programme of any London venue. It's also the venue for the annual London Film Festival staged every November. *South Bank SE1, T: 020 7928 3232, www.bfi.org.uk/nft*

Prince Charles Cinema ❷ 3F
Shows a mixture of new releases, cult classics and art-house flicks and offers cheaper seats than the other Leicester Square-area cinemas. *Lisle Street WC2, T: 020 7494 3654, www.princecharlescinema.com*

Odeon Leicester Square and Odeon West End ❷ 3F
Leicester Square WC2, T: 0871 22 44 007, www.odeon.co.uk

Vue West End ❷ 4F
Leicester Square WC2, T: 08712 240 240, www.myvue.com

Night Clubs

Fabric ❶ 2G
Huge venue, considered to be one of the best clubs in London despite the lack of big-name DJs. *77a Charterhouse Street EC1, T: 020 7336 8898, www.fabriclondon.com*

Heaven ❷ 4G
Traditionally a gay club, now popular with everyone. *Under the Arches, Villiers Street WC2, T: 020 7930 202, www.heaven-london.com*

Ministry of Sound ❶ 5G
The super-famous Ministry attracts all the top DJs and releases multi-million-selling dance CDs. *103 Gaunt Street SE1, T: 0870 060 0010, www.ministryofsound.co.uk*

Pacha ❶ 5D
London's version of the legendary Ibizan nightspot is in a converted 1920s' dance hall. The decor is all swathes of marble and Victorian wood. *Terminus Place, Victoria SW1, T: 020 7833 3139, www.pachalondon.com*

Spectator Sport

Cricket

Lord's ❶ 1C

Near Regent's Park and regarded by many as the 'home of cricket'.
St John's Wood NW8,
T: 020 7432 1066, www.lords.org

The Oval ❶ 6F

Kennington SW11, T: 020 7582 6660,
www.surreycricket.com

Football

Wembley Stadium (off map)

International matches will be played at the newly rebuilt and redesigned Wembley Stadium. 'The Church of Football' is scheduled to be open for its first congregation by 2007, although completion has been seriously delayed.
Empire Way, Wembley, Middlesex,
T: 020 8795 9000,
www.wembleystadium.com

Rugby Union

Twickenham (off map)

England plays its home matches at Twickenham. Every year, England, Wales, Scotland, Ireland, France and Italy compete in the Six Nations tournament. *Rugby Road, Twickenham, Middlesex,*
T: 020 8831 6527, www.rfu.com

Tennis

All England Lawn Tennis and Croquet Club (off map)

Wimbledon is home of strawberries and cream, interminable rain delays and mile-long queues. Centre and No.1 Court tickets are allocated by

Twickenham, the home of English Rugby

public ballot some six months prior. Queuing on match day takes hours and only entitles you to access the outer courts. Sometimes return tickets are available from 2pm onwards.
Church Road, Wimbledon SW19,
T: 020 8971 2473, www.wimbledon.org

Participation Sport

Ice Skating

The most picturesque is the outdoor rink set up at Somerset House, open over the Christmas period (*see p.12*).

Broadgate Ice Rink ❶ 2H

Broadgate Circus, Eldon Street EC2,
T: 020 7505 4068,
www.broadgateice.co.uk

Swimming

Serpentine Lido ❶ 4C

Sunbathe or dip in the outdoor pool in central London. *Open 10am-6pm daily Jun-Sep. Hyde Park,*
T: 020 7706 3422
T: 020 7352 6985,
www.serpentinelido.com

london places to eat and drink

Britain is fast gaining a reputation for her culinary skills and it's London, as always, that's leading the way. Thanks to unprecedented expansion in the 1980s and 90s, London now has a restaurant scene fit to rival any in the world, with something to suit every taste and budget. This growth has been helped, in no small measure, by the city's great ethnic diversity, which has bred a corresponding culinary variety. So, whatever your preference, be it for curry, noodles, sushi, pasta, steak or fish'n'chips, you'll find the restaurant to suit you somewhere in the capital.

taste it places to eat and drink

Price Guide
Per person without drinks
£ = less than £15
££ = less than £40
£££ = more than £40

African

Calabash £-££ ❷3G
Sample the delights of couscous, groundnut stew and *yassa* at this excellent restaurant. The cuisine is authentic African with a splendid selection of African wines. *Africa Centre, 38 King Street WC2, T: 020 7836 1976, www.africacentre.org.uk*

American

Joe Allen £-££ ❷3H
Upmarket diner serving transatlantic favourites such as eggs benedict, steaks and fried chicken, and popular with West End actors: hence all the theatre memorabilia on the walls. *13 Exeter Street WC2, T: 020 7836 0651, www.joeallenrestaurant.com*

Argentinian

The Gaucho Grill ££ ❷4E
Specialises, as you'd expect, in big fat juicy steaks. *19 Swallow Street W1, T: 020 7734 4040.*
Branches: *89 Sloane Avenue SW3, T: 020 7584 9901; 125 Chancery Lane WC2, T: 020 7242 7727, www.gaucho-grill.com*

British

Boisdale ££ ❶5D
Serves traditional Scottish dishes – haggis, beer-battered fish, tatties and neeps, as well as carefully sourced premium-quality beef – and stocks

Bluebird bar and restaurant

It's a Wine World
Acting as a sort of shrine to wine, Vinopolis ❶5D sits on the South Bank close to the Globe Theatre (*see p.12*). Take a tour through the wine regions of the world, sample a fine vintage in Wine Wharf, buy a bottle or two in the extensive gourmet shop and to complete your experience, eat in the celebrated Cantina Vinopolis. *Open daily, late Mon, Fri, Sat. Guided tours. No 1 Bank End SE1. T: 0870 241 4040 www.vinopolis.co.uk*

more than 200 varieties of whisky – the best selection in London. *13-15 Eccleston Street SW1, T: 020 7730 6922; Branch: Swedeland Court, 202 Bishopsgate EC2M, T: 020 7283 1763, www.boisdale.co.uk*

Porters ££ ❷ 3G
A veritable temple of pies and one of the great bastions of British cooking, Porters' menu features everything from the traditional steak and kidney pie to the more unusual chicken and broccoli. *17 Henrietta Street WC2, T: 020 7836 6466, www.porters.uk.com*

St John £-££ ❶ 2G
Not for the faint-hearted. This very English establishment is the sort of place where Dr Johnson would have felt entirely at home. Dedicated to serving up all types of meat – as supplied by the meat market at Smithfield next door – it's particularly famed for its offal dishes but has others to suit the more squeamish diner. It also runs the nearby bar-bakery 'St John Bread & Wine'. *26 St John Street EC1, T: 020 7251 0848, www.stjohnrestaurant.co.uk*

Modern British

Bluebird ££-£££ ❶ 6C
This is one of the best of Terence Conran's mighty chain of London gastro-domes; the complex boasts a well-respected restaurant, a scrumptious deli, a café and bar. *350 King's Road SW3, T: 020 7559 1000, www.conran-restaurants.co.uk*

Fifteen ££-£££ ❶ 1G
Thanks to the accompanying TV series, Jamie Oliver's 'charity' restaurant, in which he trains underprivileged kids to work in his kitchen, is probably the city's best known. The food is sumptuous, if expensive, but all the profits go to the charity. It's generally booked up months in advance but they might be able to squeeze you in at short notice at the downstairs trattoria. *Westland Place N1, T: 0871 330 1515, www.fifteenrestaurant.com*

Gordon Ramsay £££ ❶ 6C
The extremely well-heeled restaurant of the famously temperamental chef has been showered with praise, not to mention Michelin stars. The food

is as modern and inventive as it gets. Ramsay's ever-expanding restaurant empire also includes eateries at Claridge's and the Berkeley Hotel. *68-69 Royal Hospital Road SW3, T: 020 7352 4441, www.gordonramsay.com*

The Ivy £££ ❷ 3F
The ultimate celeb hang-out (where the paparazzi are seemingly permanently encamped) is also an exquisite restaurant (regularly voted the capital's favourite) offering a simple, beautifully crafted menu. You'll need to book The Ivy weeks in advance and it would, of course,

Entrance to The Ivy

help if you're the star of your own TV show. *1 West Street WC2, T: 020 7836 4751.*

Oxo Tower Restaurant £££ ❶ 4G

Set beneath the grand 1930s art deco tower, one of the capital's great landmarks stands alongside the Thames, providing fantastic views out over London and a good menu to boot. The food is made up of a hotch-potch of influences –

> **Did You Know?**
> That the Oxo Tower's distinctive design was created to circumvent the strict anti-advertising laws in place in the 1930s?

Mediterranean, French, and British. *Oxo Tower, Barge House Street SE1, T: 020 7803 3888, www.oxotower.co.uk*

People's Palace ££ ❶ 4F

With its sweeping views and excellent modern-ish menu, this has become a favourite haunt of theatre- and concert-goers. *Closed for refurbishment until 2007. Level 3, Royal Festival Hall SE1, T: 020 7928 9999.*

Quaglino's £££ ❷ 5D

Another of London's trendy, star-studded eateries owned by the Conran empire, this serves expertly prepared cuisine in its beautifully appointed sunken dining room. *16 Bury Street SW1, T: 020 7930 6767.*

Rhodes 24 £££ ❶ 3H

The celebrated TV chef's restaurant offers the twin delights of spectacular views (it's located on the 24th floor of one of the capital's highest buildings) and a menu dedicated to updating classic British cuisine – braised oxtail cottage pie, cockle and leek casserole, jam roly poly and so

on. Last orders are at 9pm. *Tower 42, Old Broad St EC2, T: 020 7877 7703, www.garyrhodes.com*

Catering for Kids

Many restaurants now go out of their way to welcome families, with funpacks and games for the kids and well-thought-out children's menus. Some even go so far as to lay on entertainment at weekends in the shape of magicians or clowns. All branches of **TGI Friday's**, **Café**

Toys in the window, Rainforest Café

Rouge, Maxwell's and **Smollensky's** are particularly family friendly, as is the **Rainforest Café** (❷ 2F) where you get to eat your burgers and fries in a replica jungle setting while animatronic creatures chatter away in the background.
20 Shaftesbury Avenue W1,
T: 020 7434 3111,
www.therainforestcafe.co.uk,

Chinese

There are Chinese restaurants on almost every London high street. For the best and most diverse Chinese cuisine, however, there's only really one place to go – Gerrard Street and Lisle Street (❷ 2F), two small roads just to the north of Leicester Square which together make up London's exotic Chinatown district.

Chuen Cheng Ku ££ ❷ 3F
This cavernous restaurant boasts the largest menu in Chinatown, which, considering the competition, is quite some claim. The dim sum (Chinese dumplings) are particularly excellent and are served from trolleys from

lunchtime onwards, along with an endless supply of green tea.
17 Wardour Street W1,
T: 020 7437 1398,
www.chuenchengku.co.uk

Golden Harvest £ ❷ 3F
Simple, beautifully prepared food full of delightful spices and flavours, with no monosodium glutamate in sight. *17 Lisle Street WC2,*
T: 020 7287 3822.

Fish 'n' Chips

Previously held up as a symbol of everything that was wrong with British food – greasy, fatty, bland – this great dish has undergone something of a post-modern re-evaluation of late. As a happy consequence, the number of upmarket fish and chip restaurants has increased dramatically in London during recent years.

Livebait ££ ❶ 4F
With decor as fresh and pure as the day's catch, it's difficult to go wrong here. They serve everything from classic fish and chips to more

Elevated Eating
Gaze at the London skyline in the sixth-floor Café on Level 7 at the Tate Modern (*see p.13*), the Studio Lounge at Waterstone's in Piccadilly (*see p.23*), the Fifth Floor restaurant at Harvey Nichols (*see p.20*), the People's Palace at the South Bank (*see left*), Rhodes 24 on the 24th floor of Tower 42 (*see left*) and, if you can afford it, the Oxo Tower Restaurant (*see left*), a magical night-time dining experience. If your budget is tight, there's a free viewing platform next door to the Oxo Tower Restaurant.

adventurous fare – crab and prawn linguine perhaps. Great seafood platters. *43 The Cut SE1, T: 020 7928 7211, www.santeonline.co.uk/livebait/*

Rock and Sole Plaice ££ ❷ 2G
Established in 1871, this is London's oldest fish and chip shop and one of the best. It serves all the staples – cod, rock, haddock and plaice – with particularly good chips. Book at the weekends Bring your own wine. *47 Endell Street WC2, T: 020 7836 3785, www.rockandsoleplaice.com*

French

Bibendum £££ ❶ 5C
Superb French cuisine served up in a former Michelin-tyre factory, the whole presided over by Terence Conran, the man who has perhaps done more than any other to shape the modern London dining experience. *Michelin House, 81 Fulham Road SW3, T: 020 7581 5817, www.bibendum.co.uk*

L'Escargot £££ ❷ 2F
This bastion of garlic (now owned by chef Marco Pierre White) has been feeding the denizens of Soho and further afield with tasty Gallic fare (including, of course, the eponymous snails) for decades now. Upstairs in the Picasso Room you will find a decent-value set-lunch menu. *48 Greek Street W1, T: 020 7437 2679, www.lescargotrestaurant.co.uk*

Indian

Curry has been called the nation's favourite dish. London boasts plenty of first-rate establishments in which to sample the culinary delights of the subcontinent in all its fiery spiciness.

Famous façade of L'Escargot

Cinnamon Club £££ ❶ 5E
Occupying the grand open spaces of the former Westminster Library, the extremely well-to-do Cinnamon Club comes across as a mix between a gentlemen's club, a French deli and a (very) upmarket curry house, and is very popular with politicians and media types. There's a nice quiet bar beneath the main restaurant. *Great Smith Street SW1, T: 020 7222 2555, www.cinnamonclub.com*

Tamarind ££ ❷ 5C
This Michelin-starred popular restaurant offers what could perhaps be described as Modern Indian, where the emphasis is on the presentation and re-interpretation of regional dishes to give them a distinctive style. *20 Queen Street W1, T: 020 7629 3561, www.tamarindrestaurant.com*

Veeraswamy ££ ❷ 4E
One of central London's best curry houses has just been transformed into a luxuriously chic spot to unwind after a hard day's shopping. *99 Regent Street, T: 020 7734 1401, www.veeraswamy.com*

Italian

Passione ££ **1** 3E

Upmarket pastas and pizzas in a groovy, oh-so-trendy setting in the heart of TV-land. Spot the media men as they lunch. *10 Charlotte Street W1, T: 020 7636 2833, www.passione.co.uk*

The dining room at Veeraswamy

Japanese

Nobu £££ **2** 6B

As trendy as they come, this hybrid Japanese-American affair usually gathers together a smattering of celebrities come the weekend. Expect excellent cuisine and stark

modern decor. Booking essential. *Metropolitan Hotel, 19 Old Park Lane W1, T: 020 7447 4747.*

Wagamama £ **2** 3G, **1** 1G, **2** 3H

Diners eat fast food Japanese-style, with fresh noodle and rice dishes, at long shared tables. No booking required. **Branches:** *10a Lexington Street W1, T: 020 7292 0990; 1a Tavistock St WC2, T: 020 7836 3330; 4a Streatham St, T: 020 7323 9223; 101a Wigmore Street W1, T: 020 7409 0111; 14a Irving Street WC2, T: 020 7839 2323; Royal Festival Hall SE, T: 020 7021 0877, www.wagamama.com*

Yo! Sushi £ **2** 2F, **2** 3E, **1** 4C, **1** 3B, **2** 1F, **1** 4H

Select sushi from a conveyor belt and be served by the robotic drinks waiter. **Branches:** *52 Poland Street W1, T: 020 7287 0443; 19 Rupert Street W1 T: 020 7434 2724: Harvey Nichols (see p.20); Paddington Station; myhotel Bloomsbury (see p.57); 95 Farringdon Road EC1, T: 020 7841 0785; County Hall, Belvedere Road SE1, T: 020 7928 8871, www.yosushi.com*

Moroccan

Momo ££ **2** 2E

One of the best middle eastern restaurants in the city. All the couscous and tajines you can eat at this upmarket, spectacularly trendy Moroccan restaurant with authentic lanterns, cushions and brass tables. Listen to the resident DJs (you can even buy their CDs) in the bar, or enjoy pastries in the tearoom. *25 Heddon Street W1, T: 020 7434 4040, www.momoresto.com*

Modern eating at Yo! Sushi

Vegetarian Restaurants

Most menus have meat-free options, or try one of the veggie cafés below:

Vegetarian dishes to tempt you

Food for Thought ❷2G
31 Neal Street WC2,
T: 020 7836 0239.

Mildreds ❷3E
45 Lexington Street W1,
T: 020 7494 1634,
www.mildreds.co.uk

The Place Below ❶3G
Delicious soups and hot dishes in a crypt and opens 7.30am-3.30pm.
St-Mary-le-Bow Church EC2,
T: 020 7329 0789,
www.theplacebelow.co.uk

Early morning at Bar Italia

Cafés

Bar Italia £ ❷3F
Cheery Soho café-bar open 24 hours a day from Monday to Saturday and on Sunday from 7am-4am. So, if you're feeling rather peckish at 3am, this is the place to head for. *22 Frith Street W1, T: 020 7437 4520.*

Brick Lane Bagel Bake £ ❶2H
Open 24 hours a day, this serves the best bagels in London. The salmon-and-cream cheese variety is particularly recommended. *159 Brick Lane E1, T: 020 7729 0616.*

Café in the Crypt £ ❷4G
Spooky subterranean café housed in the crypt of St Martin-in-the-Fields Church. It has a jolly atmosphere, despite its dungeon-esque locale, and the menu features lots of vegetarian choices. *St Martin-in-the-Fields Church, Duncannon Street WC2, T: 020 7766 1158, www2.stmartin-in-the-fields.org*

Coffee Gallery £ ❷1G
Handy for the British Museum, this bright and cheerful coffee shop does very reasonably priced snacks, cakes and sandwiches. *23 Museum Street WC1, T: 020 7436 0455.*

Franx Snack Bar £ ❷2G
Cheery 'greasy spoon' for a proper full English breakfast – eggs, bacon, sausages, tomatoes and a fried slice *192 Shaftesbury Avenue WC2, T: 020 7836 7989.*

ICA Café £ ❷5F
This arts-centre café is reasonably

price, stays open late (1am) and gets very crowded. *12 Carlton House Terrace, The Mall SW1, T: 020 7930 8619.*

Pâtisserie Valerie £ ❷ 3F

Stocks a wonderful array of treats.
Branches: *44 Old Compton Street W1, T: 020 7437 3466; 105 Marylebone High Street W1, T: 020 7935 6240; 8 Russell Street WC2, T: 020 7240 0064; 215 Brompton Road SW1, T: 020 7823 9971, www.patisserie-valerie.co.uk*

Desserts at Patisserie Valerie

Afternoon Tea

The following hotels and establishments offer afternoon or 'high' tea – which should usually

---

Pie and Mash

For a true taste of London, eschew the fancy eateries and head to south and east London, homes of the pie and mash shop. The menu is simple: pies (steak or eel, or sometimes a veggie option), served with mash and a parsley sauce called 'liquor'. Try the following:
Goddard's, *Greenwich Church Street SE10.*
G. Kelly's, *41 Bethnal Green Road E2.*
F. Cooke's, *Hoxton Street N1.*
J. Kelly, *150 Roman Road E2.*
Manze's, *87 Tower Bridge Road SE1.*

---

involve delicate sandwiches, scones, cakes, clotted cream and strawberry jam – served in opulent surroundings for around £20 per head in the late afternoon. A jacket and tie are essential dress for the men and it's advisable to book well in advance – weeks in the case of the ever-popular Ritz or Savoy.

Brown's Hotel ££ ❷ 4D

30 Albemarle Street W1, T: 020 7493 6020, www.brownshotel.com

Claridge's Hotel ££ ❷ 3C

Brook Street W1, T: 020 7629 8860, www.claridges.co.uk

Fortnum and Mason Fountain Restaurant ££ ❷ 5E

181 Piccadilly W1, T: 020 7734 8040.

Ritz Hotel ££ ❷ 5D

150 Piccadilly W1, T: 020 7493 8181, www.theritzlondon.com

Savoy Hotel ££ ❷ 4H

The Strand WC2, T: 020 7836 4343, www.savoy-group.co.uk

The Ritz at Christmas time

Pubs & Bars

Nights out in Britain are bound to include a trip to the pub; London is no exception. Nowadays there are three categories of drinking establishment: the traditional pub, cosy, friendly and probably serving ale; the chain pub, large, garish and lager-dominated; and the bar, trendy, sophisticated, noisy and keen on cocktails and wine.

While most pub-goers opt for cold fizzy lager, it's worth trying a sup of ale: darker, tastier and bitter. Recent changes to the law mean pubs can stay open 24 hours if they choose.

The Coal Hole

The Anchor ❶ 4G

With an outdoor terrace overlooking the river, this ancient pub provides an ideal spot to wind down after watching a performance at the Globe (*see p.12*). It was supposedly the location from where Samuel Pepys watched the Fire of London, before the pub itself burned down. *34 Park Street, Bankside SE1, T: 020 7407 1577.*

Bierodrome ❶ 3E

Bar owned by the people behind Belgo; warm and friendly with more than 200 types of beer. *67 Kingsway WC2, T: 020 7242 7469.*
Branch: *173-174 Upper Street N1, T: 020 7226 5835, www.belgo-restaurants.com*

Cantaloupe ❶ 3E

Lively, fun and often extremely crowded modern bar. One of the places to be seen. *35-42 Charlotte Street EC2, T: 020 7613 4411, www.cantaloupe.co.uk*

Coach and Horses ❷ 3F

This pub is small and creaky but undeniably very, very London with cheap pints and sandwiches. *29 Greek Street W1, T: 020 7437 5920.*

The Coal Hole ❷ 4H

Where Gilbert and Sullivan used to get together to discuss their latest productions, the Coal Hole attracts its fair share of thespians. It's on three levels and gets very crowded. *91 The Strand, T: 020 7379 9883.*

George Inn ❶ 4H

Such is the historic importance of this rambling 17th-century coaching inn – it stands near the site of the Tabard Inn, where Chaucer's pilgrim gathered to tell their tales – that it has been bought by the National Trust. *Talbot Yard, 77 Borough High Street SE1, T: 020 7407 2056.*

Name that Pub

Many of the names of traditional pubs – Lamb and Flag, Hoop and Grapes – were specially devised so as to be easy to represent pictorially on the pub sign, thus allowing illiterate drinkers to find the right hostelry.

Gordon's Wine Bar ❷ 5G

Hugely popular subterranean wine bar with the wine served from huge barrels. Descending the stairs, it feels like entering a secret society; once inside it is relaxed but busy. *47 Villiers Street WC2, T: 020 7930 1408.*

Hoop and Grapes ❶ 3H

This charming little pub is housed in one of the oldest buildings in the capital (c.1500) and was one of the few to escape the Great Fire. *17 Aldgate High Street EC3, T: 020 7265 5171.*

The Lamb and Flag

Lamb and Flag ❷ 3G

Tucked up an alleyway near Covent Garden, this age-old pub (supposedly one of the oldest in London) is always packed with people. *33 Rose Street WC2, T: 020 7497 9504.*

Market Porter ❶ 4G

If you fancy a convivial pint at 6am, this is the place to come. It opens its doors early for the benefit of the traders at nearby Borough Market. It also featured in the movies *Lock, Stock...* and *Mission Impossible.* *9 Stoney Street SE1, T: 020 7407 2495.*

Mash ❷ 2D

One of the better modern bars, Mash has a style all its own. It can get very crowded at the weekend. *19-21 Great Portland Street W1, T: 020 7637 5555.*

Pitcher & Piano ❷ 2E

Extremely popular Soho branch of the now ubiquitous chain, housed in a Grade II listed building. *69-70 Dean Street W1, T: 020 7434 3585, www.pitcherandpiano.com*

The Pitcher and Piano

Ye Olde Cheshire Cheese ❶ 3F

This lively pub-cum-chop house first opened for business back in the 1670s and can count Dr Johnson, Dickens and Mark Twain among its former patrons. *145 Fleet Street EC4, T: 020 7353 6170.*

Vertigo42 ❶ 3H

Book in advance to enjoy a drink (and the views) looking over London from the 42nd floor of Tower 42. A snack and seafood bar, it has room for just 70 people. *Tower 42, 25 Old Broad St EC2, T: 020 7877 7842, www.vertigo42.co.uk*

london practical information

From a tiny settlement on the banks of the River Thames, London has grown over the course of the last 2,000 years into one of the largest cities in the world, a vast metropolis of more than a thousand square miles that provides a home to more than seven million people. Despite its size, there's no reason to feel daunted at the prospect of visiting London. Most of its main tourist attractions are actually located in or around Central London, which can be easily navigated on foot. What follows will hopefully help you to get to grips with the finer details of London living – getting there, the transport system, currency and so on.

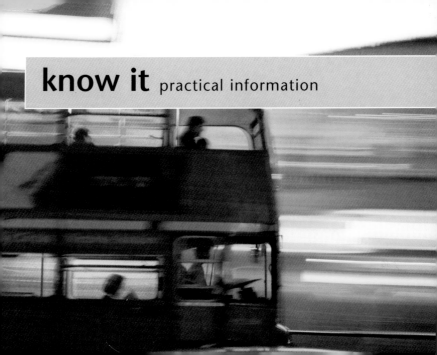

know it practical information

Tourist Information

London Tourist Board
Offices are found in Victoria,
Liverpool Street and Waterloo
Stations, and at Heathrow
Airport. *T: 020 7932 2000,*
www.visitlondon.com

Visit Britain ❷ 4E
Provides maps and operates a
countrywide hotel booking
service, as well as selling the
London Pass (*see below*).
1 Regent Street W1,
www.visitbritain.com

London Pass
The London Pass gives free
entry to 50 of London's
attractions, commission-free
currency exchange, free
internet access and discounts
at restaurants. It costs:
1 day – adult £30, child £18;
2 days – adult £42, child £29;
3 days – adult £52, child £34;
6 days – adult £72, child £48.
www.londonpass.com

Arrivals by Air

As befits a city of its size and
status, London is served by five
airports, but you're most likely
to touch down at one of the two
largest: Heathrow and Gatwick.
The national carrier is
British Airways: *T: 08705 511 155,*
www.britishairways.com

Heathrow

Heathrow, the busiest airport in the
world, is located 15 miles (24km)
west of London. There are several
options for travelling into central
London.

Airbus Heathrow Shuttle
Shuttle buses run every 30 minutes
to stops in the city centre from
5.30am-9.30pm. Cost £7 single,
£12 return. Under 15s travel free.
T: 08705 757 747, www.airbus.co.uk

Heathrow Express ❶3B
Trains run every 15 minutes between
the airport and Paddington Station,
which connects to the tube. The
journey takes 15 minutes and costs
£13. *T: 0845 600 1515,*
www.heathrowexpress.com

Check-in at Heathrow

Taxi
The most comfortable, convenient
and most expensive option for
getting in to town. A black taxi from
Heathrow to central London will co[?]
in the region of £30-35 (more after
8pm). Taxi ranks are outside of the
arrivals halls.
Radio Taxis: *T: 020 7272 0272.*

Underground (Tube) ❹
The Piccadilly Line connects
Heathrow with central London
between 5am and midnight daily.
The journey takes between 40
minutes and over an hour. A single
adult ticket costs £4 – it's not
recommended in rush hours when
the carriages become overcrowded.
www.tfl.gov.uk

Gatwick

London's second largest airport is 25 miles (48km) south of central London. **Airport Enquiries**: T: 0870 000 2468.

The following options exist for travelling into London:

Gatwick Express ❶ 5D

Trains run every 15 minutes from 6am–12 midnight daily direct to Victoria Station, and then every half an hour through the night (single £14). The journey takes just over half an hour. A slow service stops at Croydon and Clapham Junction. T: 0845 850 1530, www.gatwickexpress.co.uk

Gatwick Express at Victoria

National Express

Operates between 3.30am–11.30pm. A single ticket costs £8, a return £12. The journey to Victoria can take up to two hours. T: 08705 757 747, www.nationalexpress.com

Taxi

A black cab to London costs about £50 to £60 and takes over an hour.

Smaller Airports

London City

4 miles (6 km) east of the city. A shuttle bus runs to Liverpool Street every few minutes (30 minutes/ £6.00). T: 020 7646 0088, www.londoncityairport.com

Luton

32 miles (50km) north of London and linked by direct train to Victoria Station (one hour/£12.40). T: 01582 405 100, www.london-luton.co.uk

Stansted

The Stansted Express links the airport with Liverpool Street Station (45 minutes/£12.50). T: 0870 0000 303, www.stanstedexpress.co.uk

Arriving in London

By Coach ❶ 5D

Victoria Coach Station services the UK and Europe. It's a short walk to Victoria Station, from where you can catch trains and tubes. *52 Grosvenor Gardens SW1, T: 08705 808 080, www.nationalexpress.com*

By Eurostar ❶ 4F

Super-speedy Eurostar trains bring continental visitors from Paris and Brussels through the Channel Tunnel to Waterloo Station. The full journey takes around three hours, of which 25 minutes is spent in the tunnel itself. Waterloo links to the underground and has a taxi rank.

Eurostar at Waterloo

Waterloo International Terminal SE1, T: 08705 186 186, www.eurostar.com

By Train

There are direct rail services to London from all Britain's major cities. **Information:** T: 08457 48 49 50, www.nationalrail.co.uk

Getting Around

London Transport Enquiries

T: 020 7222 1234, www.tfl.gov.uk

Travel Cards

Travel and Oyster Pre Pay cards permit unlimited travel on London's buses, tubes and trains. A one-day **travelcard** covering zones 1-2 (most of the sights are here) costs adults £6.20, and children £3.10 Mon-Fri. An adult off-peak travelcard can be bought after 9.30am and on Saturdays and Sundays for £4.90. Three-day cards are also available. Alternatively you can purchase an **Oyster Card** (for a refundable £3 deposit) and top it up as you go at stations and online; individual fare prices then work out cheaper than standard ones.

Buses

Bus routes cover much of Central London but congestion problems make them less reliable than the tube during peak hours. They are good for sightseeing and cheap: a flat fare of £1.50 per journey. Buy a ticket from the driver. Day services run from 5am-12 midnight, after which N-prefixed nightbuses take over, most departing from Trafalgar Square (❷3G).

Underground/Tube ❹

The underground railway network (or 'tube') is the quickest way of getting around London. With 12

An underground sign

Traditional London bus

colour-coded interconnecting lines traversing the city, you're always close to a tube station. The service runs 5am-12 midnight daily.

Docklands Light Railway

In the Docklands and South East London, the tube is augmented by the DLR, a driverless overground monorail that joins up with the underground at Bank and Tower Hill

Taxis

Black Taxis

London's iconic black cabs are not cheap but they are reliable – potential taxi drivers must commit every London street to memory

A black taxi

before they qualify for their badge, which can take two years. Because each journey is metered, you know exactly what you owe. A taxi whose orange 'For Hire' sign is lit up can be hailed on the street.

Minicabs

Minicabs are cheaper than black cabs, but drivers don't have to pass tests so their local knowledge may be scant. Most minicabs don't have meters so agree a price beforehand.

Congestion Charge

If you want to explore the city by car, you have to pay for the privilege: a congestion charge of £8 per day (or £10 if you pay the following day), Monday-Friday from 7am-6.30pm, is in effect from Grand Union Canal in North Kensington down to Holland Park along Chelsea Embankment, Elephant & Castle in the south, Tower Bridge in the east, to King's Cross in the north. Entry points to the zone are marked with a giant red C on the road. Failure to pay will result in a £50 or £100 fine. The charge can be paid up by phone, online or at certain selected shops. *T: 0845 900 1234, www.cclondon.com*

Climate

London is not always cold and foggy. The winters are cold; temperatures drop below zero, but conditions are damp rather than icy. Summer has plenty of sunny days as well as rainy ones. Average temperatures in Jul-Aug are 22°C (75°F), dropping to 7°C (44°F) during Dec-Jan.

Disabled Access

Holiday Care Service

Details of accessible accommodation and attractions. *T: 0845 124 9971, www.holidaycare.org.uk*

Embassies

Australian High Commission ❶ 3F

Australia House WC2,
T: 020 7379 4334,
www.australia.org.uk

Canadian High Commission ❷ 3B

1 Grosvenor Square W1,
T: 020 7258 6600,
www.canada.org.uk

Irish Embassy ❷ 7B

17 Grosvenor Place SW1,
T: 020 7235 2171,
foreignaffairs.gov.ie

US Embassy ❷ 4B

24 Grosvenor Square W1,
T: 020 7499 9000,
www.usembassy.org.uk

Emergencies

The following hospitals have accident and emergency departments should you require:

Chelsea & Westminster ❶ 6B

369 Fulham Road SW10,
T: 020 8746 8000,
www.chelwest.nhs.uk

Guy's ❶ 4H

St Thomas' Street SE1,
T: 020 7188 7188,
www.guysandstthomas.nhs.uk

Ambulance, fire and police:
T: 999.

A London ambulance

Lost Property

Transport for London
Lost Property Office ❶ 2D
Open 8.30am till 4pm, Mon-Fri.
200 Baker Street NW1,
T: 020 7486 2496/ 0845 330 9882,
www.tfl.gov.uk/tfl/ph_lost.shtml

Money & Banks

Banks and Bureaux de Change

The banks all operate cash dispensers for 24-hour withdrawal with Maestro symbol and credit cards. Each bank operates a bureau de change, with more found at airports and stations.

Currency

Britain's currency is the pound (£), divided into 100 pence (p). There are eight coin denominations: 1p, 2p, 5p, 10p, 20p, 50p, £1 and £2, and four notes: £5, £10, £20, £50.

Debit and Credit Cards

The majority of shops, restaurants and services accept all major credit cards and Maestro symbol cards, although you must know your four-figure PIN number for authorisation.

Opening Hours

Bank are typically open 9.30am-5pm Mon-Fri, 9am-11.30pm Sat.

Shops usually open from 9.30am till 6 or 7pm Mon-Fri (some till 9pm Thu), 9am-5pm Sat, 11am-5pm Sun.

Pharmacies

Zafash ❶ 6B

London's only 24-hour chemist.
233 Old Brompton Road SW5,
T: 020 7373 2798.

Post Offices

Main Post Office ❷ 4G

Branches usually open Mon-Fri 9am-5.30pm, Sat 9am-1pm. Newsagents also sell stamps. It costs 32p to send a letter first class in Britain, 44p to send a postcard to Europe, 50p to worldwide destinations.
Main Branch: *Open daily 8am-8pm.*
24-28 William IV Street WC2,
T: 0845 722 3344,
www.royalmail.com

Public Holidays

Banks close on the following days:

New Year's Day *1st Jan*
Good Friday *Mar-Apr (variable)*
Easter Monday *Mar-Apr (variable)*
May Day *First Mon May*
Spring Bank Holiday *Last Mon May*

Summer Bank Holiday *Last Mon Aug*
Christmas Day *25th Dec*
Boxing Day *26th Dec*

Telephones

Public phones take coins or
phonecards, available from
newsagents and post offices.
Some booths accept credit cards.

Telephone box   *Post box*

Directory Enquiries
T: 118 500,
www.directoryenquiries.co.uk

Tours

APTG Blue Badge Guides
Expert guides. T: 020 7780 4060,
www.touristguides.org.uk

Big Bus Company
Double-decker bus tours, starting
at Marble Arch. T: 020 7233 9533,
www.bigbus.co.uk

City Cruises
The Pool of London downriver
to Greenwich. T: 020 7740 0400,
www.citycruises.com

Jack the Ripper Walks
Two-hour walks around the alleys,
passages and streets of East London.
T: 020 8530 8443,
rippertour@aol.com
www.jack-the-ripper-tour.com

London Bicycle Tour Company
T: 020 7928 6838,
www.londonbicycle.com

London Duck Tours
The amphibious vehicle tours the
roads and then drives into the river.
T: 020 7928 3132,
www.londonducktours.co.uk

London Waterbus Company
Canal trips (*see box p.9*) from
Camden Lock to Little Venice.
Apr-Sep. T: 020 7482 2260,
www.londonwaterbus.com

Original London Walks
Themed walks: 'Ghosts of the West
End', 'Princess Diana's London' etc.
T: 020 7624 3978, www.walks.com

Westminster Passenger Service Association
Trips from Westminster to Hampton
Court and Kew Gardens (*see box
p.11*). Dinner cruises available.
Apr-Oct. T: 020 7930 2062,
www.wpsa.co.uk

Internet Access

Nethouse Internet Café ❶ 2C
Open daily. *138 Marylebone
Road NW1*, T: 020 7224 7008,
www.nethousecafes.com

easyEverything ❶ 5D
24-seven web access. Nine
central branches. *9-13 Wilton
Road SW1*, T: 020 7233 8456,
www.easyeverything.com

Portobello Gold ❶ 3A
Open daily. *95-97 Portobello
Road W10*, T: 020 7460 4910,
www.portobellogold.com

directory

For locals as well as newcomers, our London directory has everything you need to get the best out of the city, from annual events to finding the best hotels and places to stay in all categories. There are suggestions for seeking out additional sightseeing attractions such as museums, art galleries, historic palaces, parks and gardens not included in earlier chapters. You'll also find ideas for further reading, listings of popular web sites and local newspapers as well as a special feature on how to understand the natives.

Key to Icons

Hotels

Room Service
Restaurant
Fully Licensed Bar
En suite Bathroom

@ Business Centre
Health Centre
Air Conditioning
P Parking

Museums

Toilets
Disabled Facilities
Refreshments
Free Admission
Guided Tours

Places to Stay

From bastions of old-world antique luxury to the latest modernist masterpieces, from comfortable to fashionable, cluttered to minimalist, exorbitant to bargain, 24-hour room service to DIY catering – London has hotels to suit all tastes and budgets. Here are some of the best. All prices are inclusive of VAT (17.5 per cent).

Luxury

Brown's £££-££££ ② 4D

A fine hotel that exudes a refined country-house ambience with oak-panelling, grandfather clocks and leather armchairs. *34 Albemarle Street W1, T: 020 7493 6020, www.brownshotel.com*

Price (per double room)
£ budget (under £100)
££ moderate (£100-£180)
£££ expensive (£180-£300)
££££ deluxe (£300+)

Charlotte Street Hotel £££ ❶ 2E

Ever-so-fashionable, the public rooms offer a pastiche of old-world English style with dark wood panelling and soft-glow lighting while the bedrooms have every modern convenience. *18 Charlotte Street W1, T: 020 7806 2000, www.charlottestreethotel.com*

Covent Garden £££-££££ ❷ 2G

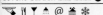

Top-of-the-range luxury combines with old-style elegance – four-poster beds, mahogany and marble right in the heart of London. *10 Monmouth Street WC2, T: 020 7806 1000, www.firmdale.com/covent.html*

Dorchester £££ ❷ 5B

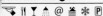

A 1930s, art deco-style hotel filled with triple-glazed, gold-leafed, velvet-cushioned opulence and long the choice of discerning film stars. *53 Park Lane W1, T: 020 7269 8888, www.dorchesterhotel.com*

The Ritz £££ ❷ 5D

Famous for its teas (*see p.45*), this is the eponymous luxury hotel; a byword for glamourous living, it is decorated in lavish rococo style with marble, gilt bronze and gold leaf. *150 Piccadilly W1, T: 020 7493 8181, www.theritzhotel.co.uk*

The Savoy ££££ ❷ 4H

London's grand stalwart hotel is filled with antique-strewn public rooms, luxurious bedrooms and great restaurants. *Strand WC2, T: 020 7836 4343, www.savoy-group.co.uk*

Chic

The Academy ££ ❷ 5B

A collection of stylish and comfortable townhouses, with a peaceful garden, near the British Museum and Tottenham Court Road. The individually designed rooms have extras such as personal business cards and crisp Egyptian cotton linen. *21 Gower Street, Bloomsbury SW7, T: 020 7631 4115, www.theetoncollection.com*

The Gore £££ ❶ 4B

Atmospheric Victorian hotel offering a combination of antique styling and modern chic. *190 Queen's Gate SW7, T: 020 7584 6601, www.gorehotel.com*

Great Eastern Hotel ££ ❶ 3H

Terence Conran's latest hotel-cum-hip urban hangout offers super-stylish rooms and four excellent restaurants. *Liverpool Street EC2, T: 020 7618 5000, www.great-eastern-hotel.co.uk*

myhotel Bloomsbury £££ ❷ 1F

'High concept' boutique hotel designed to cater to individual needs. Everyone has their own personal assistant and the bedrooms have been thoroughly Feng Shui-ed. *11-13 Bayley Street WC1, T: 020 7580 7766, www.myhotels.co.uk*

Sanderson £££-££££ **1** 3E

Philippe Starck's super-smart surreal minimalist interior is a hip, ultra-cool style-mag favourite, especially the 80-ft Long Bar. Rooms have glass walls with flowing curtains and the dreamy white theme continues into the spa and bathhouse. *50 Berners Street W1, T: 020 7300 1400, www.sandersonlondon.com*

Portobello ££-£££ **1** 3A

Cosy rooms with masses of Victoriana and colonial-style chic furnishings, near Portobello Market (see p.22). *22 Stanley Gardens W1, T: 020 7727 2777, www.portobello-hotel.co.uk*

Affordable style

Abbey Court ££ **1** 4A

Bedrooms with an antique feel and bathrooms of marble and brass. *20 Pembridge Gardens W2, T: 020 7221 7518, www.abbeycourthotel.co.uk*

Durrants ££ **2** 1B

All dark woods and leather contrasted with clean, fresh furnishings inside this former 18th-century coaching inn combine with calm, careful service. *George Street W1, T: 020 7935 8131, www.durrantshotel.co.uk*

Harlingford £ **1** 2E

Tastefully furnished in vibrant colours, the bedrooms are large and offer great value for money. Use of the adjoining tennis courts is free to hotel guests. *61-63 Cartwright Gardens WC1, T: 020 7387 1551, www.harlingfordhotel.com*

Mayflower £ **1** 5B

Oozing an elegant East-meets-West style with hand-carved beds, Egyptian cotton sheets and oriental furnishings: a great-value hotel close to Earl's Court. *26-28 Trebovir Road SW5, T: 0207 370 0991, www.mayflowerhotel.co.uk*

Pavilion Hotel £-££ **1** 3C

Eccentric hotel near Paddington station with themed rooms such as Casablanca Nights, Highland Fling and Honky Tonk Afro, popular with visiting glitterati. *34-36 Sussex Gardens W2, T: 0207 262 0905, www.pavilionhoteluk.com*

Inexpensive

base2stay £-££ **1** 5B

The clean, simply furnished, yet elegantly designed apartments offer incredible value. All have kitchenette, and rooms for one person or family rooms. *25 Courtfield Gardens SW5, T: 0207 244 2255, www.base2stay.com*

easyHotel £ **1** 5B

Compact rooms with basic facilities (many without windows) but all en suite at budget prices. As with many easy-branded items, the earlier you book, the less you pay. *14 Lexham Gardens W8, www.easyhotel.com*

Edward Lear Hotel £ 2A

A cheerful, family-run hotel occupies the former home of the famous Victorian limerick writer, Edward Lear; close to Oxford Street. *28/30 Seymour Street W1, T: 020 7402 5401, www.edlear.com*

Hotel 167 £ ❶ 6B

Simple, individually decorated bedrooms in bright colours with modern pieces and a selection of antiques. *167 Old Brompton Road SW5, T: 020 7373 0672, www.hotel167.com*

Museums

Main entries in See it *p..2–15.*

British Library ❶ 1E

Includes the Lindisfarne Gospels and a copy of the Magna Carta. *Open 9.30am-6pm (till 8pm Tue, till 5pm Sat), 11am-5pm Sun. 96 Euston Road NW1, T: 020 7412 7332, www.bl.uk*

Clink Prison Museum ❶ 4G

Exhibits on punishment and torture in medieval prisons. *Open 10am-6pm Mon-Fri, 10am-9pm Sat-Sun. 1 Clink Street SE1, T: 020 7403 0900, www.clink.co.uk*

London Canal Museum ❶ 1F

The history of London's waterways, as well as a museum of ice cream. *Open 10am-4.30pm Tue-Sun. New Wharf Road N1, T: 020 7713 0836, www.canalmuseum.org.uk*

MCC Museum ❶ 1C

The spiritual home of cricket. *Tours daily. St John's Wood Road NW8, T: 020 7616 8656, www.lords.org*

National Army Museum ❶ 6C

History of the British Army, with uniforms and model soldiers. *Open 10am-5.30pm daily. Royal Hospital Road SW3, T: 020 7730 0717, www.national-army-museum.ac.uk*

Old Operating Theatre Museum & Herb Garret ❶ 4H

The world's oldest surviving operating theatre (1822), where gruesome pre-anaesthetic operations were carried out. *Adm. Open 10.30am-5pm daily. 9A St Thomas's Street SE1, T: 020 7188 2679, www.thegarret.org.uk*

Sir John Soane's Museum ❶ 3F

Bizarre collection of art, antiques and curiosities collected in the 18th and 19th centuries by Sir John Soane. *Open 10am-5pm Tue-Sat (till 9pm 1st Tue of each month). 13 Lincoln's Inn Fields WC2, T: 020 7405 2107, www.soane.org*

Wallace Collection ❷ 1B

Collection of 18th-century French paintings and Sèvres porcelain. *Open 10am-5pm daily. Hertford House, Manchester Square W1, T: 020 7935 0687, www.wallacecollection.org*

Galleries

Find main entries in See it pp.2–15.

ICA Gallery ② 5F

♟ ♿ ☕

Varied programme of temporary modern art exhibitions. *Open 12pm-1am Tue-Sat, 12pm-11pm Sun, 12pm-10.30pm Mon. The Mall SW1, T: 020 7930 3647, www.ica.org.uk*

Guildhall Art Gallery ❶ 3G

♟ ♿ 🏛

Displays the City of London's art. *Open 10am-4pm Mon-Sat, 12pm-4pm Sun. Gresham Street EC2, T: 020 7332 1313, www.cityoflondon.gov.uk*

Royal Academy of Arts ② 4D

♟ ♿ ☕

Temporary exhibitions: its annual Summer Exhibition of contemporary art runs from June to August. *Open 10am-6pm daily (till 10pm Fri). Burlington House, Piccadilly W1, T: 020 7300 5959, www.royalacademy.org.uk*

Monuments

Banqueting House ② 6G

Originally part of Whitehall Palace, the sovereign's residence from 1530 to 1698, with elaborate ceiling fresco painted by Rubens that can be seen from the road. *Open 10am-5pm Mon-Sat. Whitehall SW1, T: 0870 751 5178, www.hrp.org.uk*

HMS Belfast ❶ 4H

♟ ♿ ☕

Enormous World War II battlecruiser, now a floating museum. *Open 10am-6pm daily (till 5pm Nov-Feb), Morgan's Lane, Tooley Street SE1, T: 020 7940 6300, www.hmsbelfast.org.uk*

Parks & Gardens

Battersea Park ❶ 6D

Boating lake, café, festival gardens, a pagoda and children's zoo. *Battersea SW11, www.batterseapark.org*

Chelsea Physic Garden ❶ 6C

Peaceful apothecaries' research garden. *Adm. Open 12 noon-5pm Wed & Sun Apr-Oct, 66 Royal Hospital Road SW3, T: 020 7352 5646, www.chelseaphysicgarden.co.uk*

Christchurch Greyfriars ❶ 3G

Delightful rose garden planted on the former site of Sir Christopher Wren's church. *Newgate Street EC1, www.christchurchtower.com*

Green Park ② 6C

Peaceful mature green park. *The Mall SW1, www.royalparks.gov.uk*

Holland Park ❶ 4A

Manicured park with an orangery, a Japanese watergarden, peacocks and a theatre (see p.31). *Kensington W8, www.rbkc.gov.uk*

Lincoln's Inn Fields ❶ 3F

17th-century garden filled with lawyers (extremely quiet considering its location), and the largest public square in London. *Holborn WC2.*

Regent's Park ❶ 1C-1D

Boating lake, tennis courts, café, open-air summer theatre and London Zoo (see p.8). *NW1, www.royalparks.gov.uk.*

Annual Events

January
London Parade (New Year's Day).
www.londonparade.co.uk

January/February
Chinese New Year Festival.
Chinatown WC1.

Easter
Oxford-Cambridge Boat Race on
the Thames. www.theboatrace.org

April
London Marathon run around
Greenwich (see p.6) and the Isle of
Dogs . www.london-marathon.co.uk
Queen's Birthday Royal Gun Salute
21st, 12 noon). Hyde Park, Tower.

May
Chelsea Flower Show (May), Physic
Garden (see left). www.rhs.org.uk

June–August
Royal Academy Summer Exhibition
(see left).
Trooping the Colour (2nd Saturday
June). The Queen's official birthday.
**Wimbledon Lawn Tennis
Championships** Two Weeks Jun-Jul.

July–September
The Proms more than 70 concerts,
(see p.8). www.bbc.co.uk/proms

August
Notting Hill Carnival (August Bank
Holiday Sun). Europe's largest.
T: 020 8964 0544, www.lnhc.org.uk

October
**Pearly Kings and Queens' Harvest
Festival** (East Enders smothered
in buttons): Second Sunday in
October www.pearlysociety.co.uk

November
Guy Fawkes/ Bonfire Night (5th).
Firework displays throughout city.
Lord Mayor's Show (second
Saturday in November, starts at
11am). EC1, www.lordmayorshow.org

December
The Christmas Lights. Trafalgar
Square, Oxford and Regent Streets,
and **New Year's Eve Celebrations**
(31st). Trafalgar Square.

Listings

For listings information, check out
the watch it section (see p.28)

Newspapers

Metro is free daily Mon-Fri from tube
stations. The London *Evening
Standard* appears late-afternoon
Mon-Fri. *The Times* and *The Guardian*
are daily Mon-Sat.

Reading

Take the Kids…London –
Joseph Fullman, *Cadogan Guides*.

London: the Biography –
Peter Akroyd, *Vintage*.
London as a living organism.

Oliver Twist – **Charles Dickens**.
One of the many London set-texts
by the great 19th-century novelist.

Websites

London Tourist Board
www.visitlondon.com

LondonTown.com
Massive discounts on hotels and
accommodation as well as
information on sightseeing.
www.londontown.com

speak it

Here are a few local words and phrases to spare any blushes during your stay in London.

All-too-common UK/US confusions
bank holiday – national holiday
Boxing Day – first week-day after Christmas (national holiday)
chemist – drugstore
dress circle (theatre) – first balcony
fags – cigarettes
fortnight – two weeks
interval – intermission
letter box or pillar box – mail-box
lift – elevator
loo/WC – toilet
rucksack – backpack
stalls – theatre seats
tap – faucet
torch – flashlight

Around London
cab rank – taxi-stand
return ticket – round trip
pavement – sidewalk
subway – pedestrian underpass
tube – subway

Babies and children
dummy – pacifier
nappy – diaper
pram – baby-carriage
pushchair – child's stroller

Clothes
anorak – windbreaker (slang: nerd)
dressing gown – robe
jumper, pullover, woolly – sweater
knickers – ladies' underpants
pants – underpants
trainers – sneakers
trousers – pants
vest – undershirt

Money
coppers – 1p and 2p coins
quid – a pound
fiver – a five pound note
tenner – a ten pound note
hole-in-the-wall – ATM

Slang
bird – woman (impolite)
bloke – man
bog – toilet
copper – policeman
fag – cigarette
knackered – extremely tired
spend a penny – go to the toilet

Cockney rhyming slang
This famous east-London dialect where words and phrases are substituted with rhyming alternatives is, despite its renown, rarely used. You may hear some of these:

Adam and Eve – believe
apples and pears – stairs
Barnet (fair) – hair
boracic (lint) – skint
brass tacks – facts
butcher's (hook) – look
china (plate) – mate, friend
cobbler's (awls) – balls, rubbish
cream-crackered – knackered, tired
daisy roots – boots
dog (and bone) – phone
dustbin lids – kids
frog and toad – road
loaf (of bread) – head
mince pies – eyes
Pete Tong – wrong
Rosy (Lea) – tea
rub-a-dub – pub
Ruby (Murray) – curry
Scarpa (flow) – go
titfer (tat) – hat
trouble 'n' strife – wife
whistle (and flute) – suit (clothes)

Compass Maps Ltd.

Written by Joe Fullman and
Fiona Quinn.

Pictures © Compass Maps
Ltd and Alan Copson, Corbis,
John Heseltine Archive, Dalí
Universe (p.6), Kensington
Palace (p.7), London
Aquarium (p.8), Museum of
London (p.9), Nik
Milner/Shakespeare's Globe
(p.12), Tate Modern (p.13),
Photodisc, Tower Bridge
Experience (p.14), V&A
Museum (p.15), Dean and
Chapter of Westminster
(p.15), B (p.23), Hamley's
(p.25), Jazz Café (p.33),
Comedy Café (p.33), Gatwick
Express (p.51).

Cover Images: imagnie.

info@popoutmaps.com
www.popout-travel.com
© 2007 Compass Maps
Ltd.

Patents Pending Worldwide.
popout™cityguide as well as
individual integrated
components including
popout™map and associated
products are the subject of
Patents Pending Worldwide

AA 3319

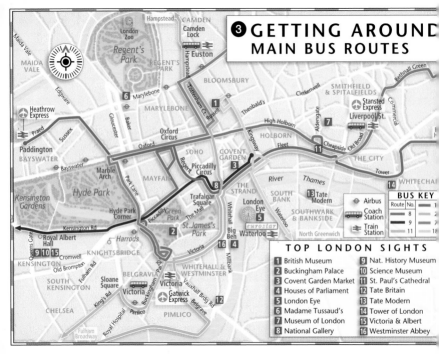

❸ GETTING AROUND
MAIN BUS ROUTES

TOP LONDON SIGHTS

1 British Museum
2 Buckingham Palace
3 Covent Garden Market
4 Houses of Parliament
5 London Eye
6 Madame Tussaud's
7 Museum of London
8 National Gallery
9 Nat. History Museum
10 Science Museum
11 St. Paul's Cathedral
12 Tate Britain
13 Tate Modern
14 Tower of London
15 Victoria & Albert
16 Westminster Abbey

BUS KEY

		Route No.	
			1
		8	2
		9	7
		11	18

Airbus
Coach Station
Train Station